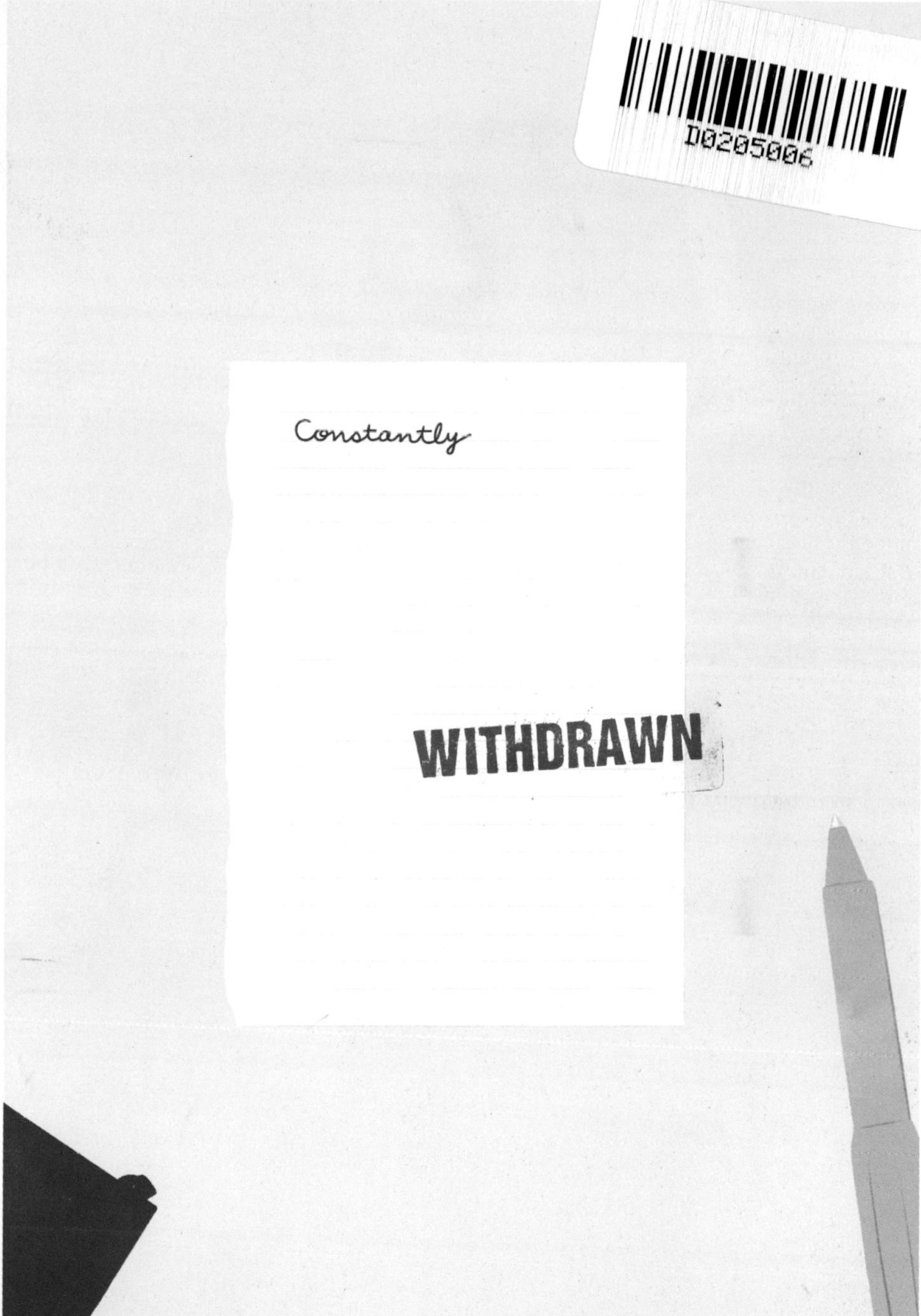
Constantly

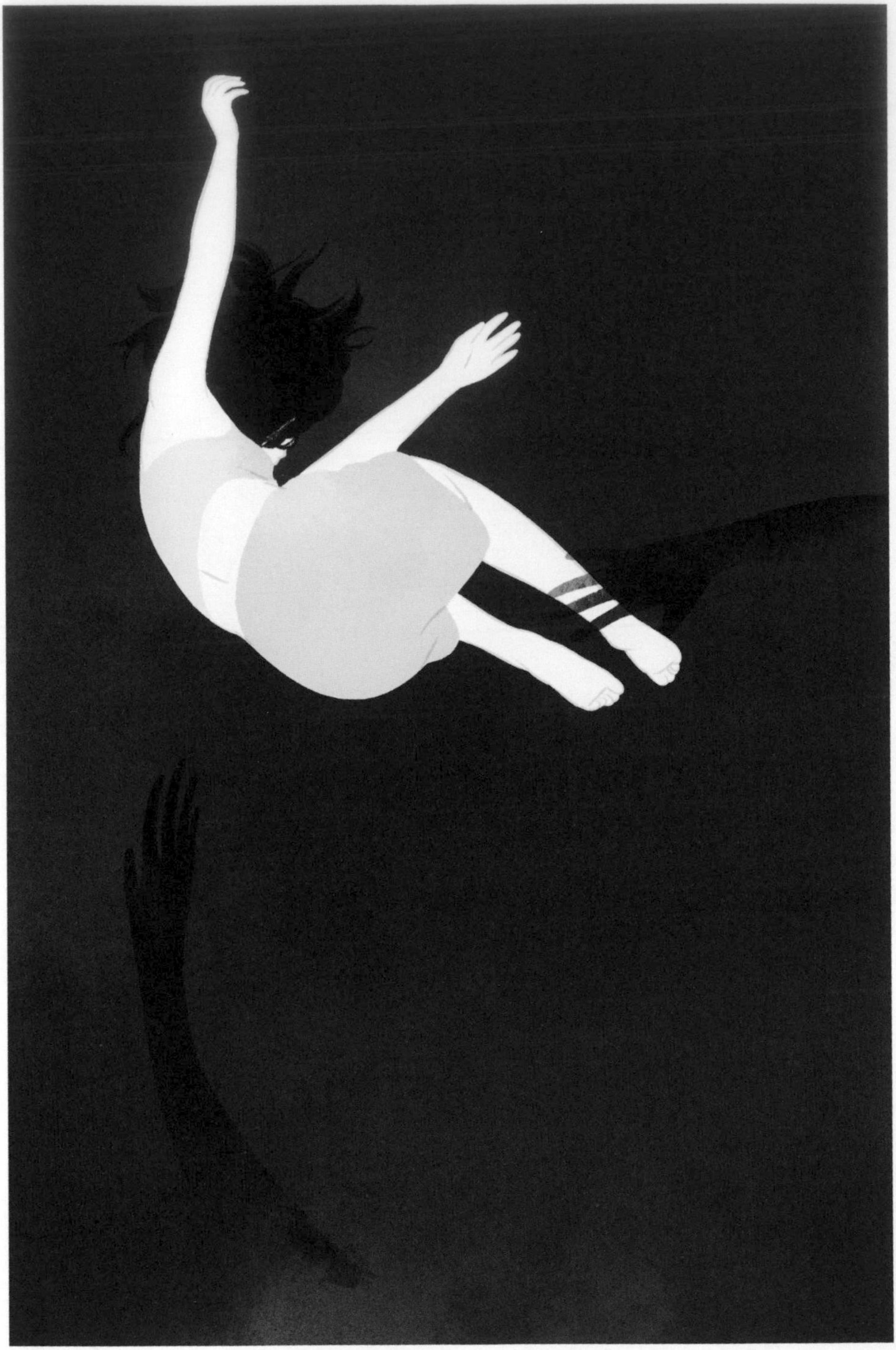

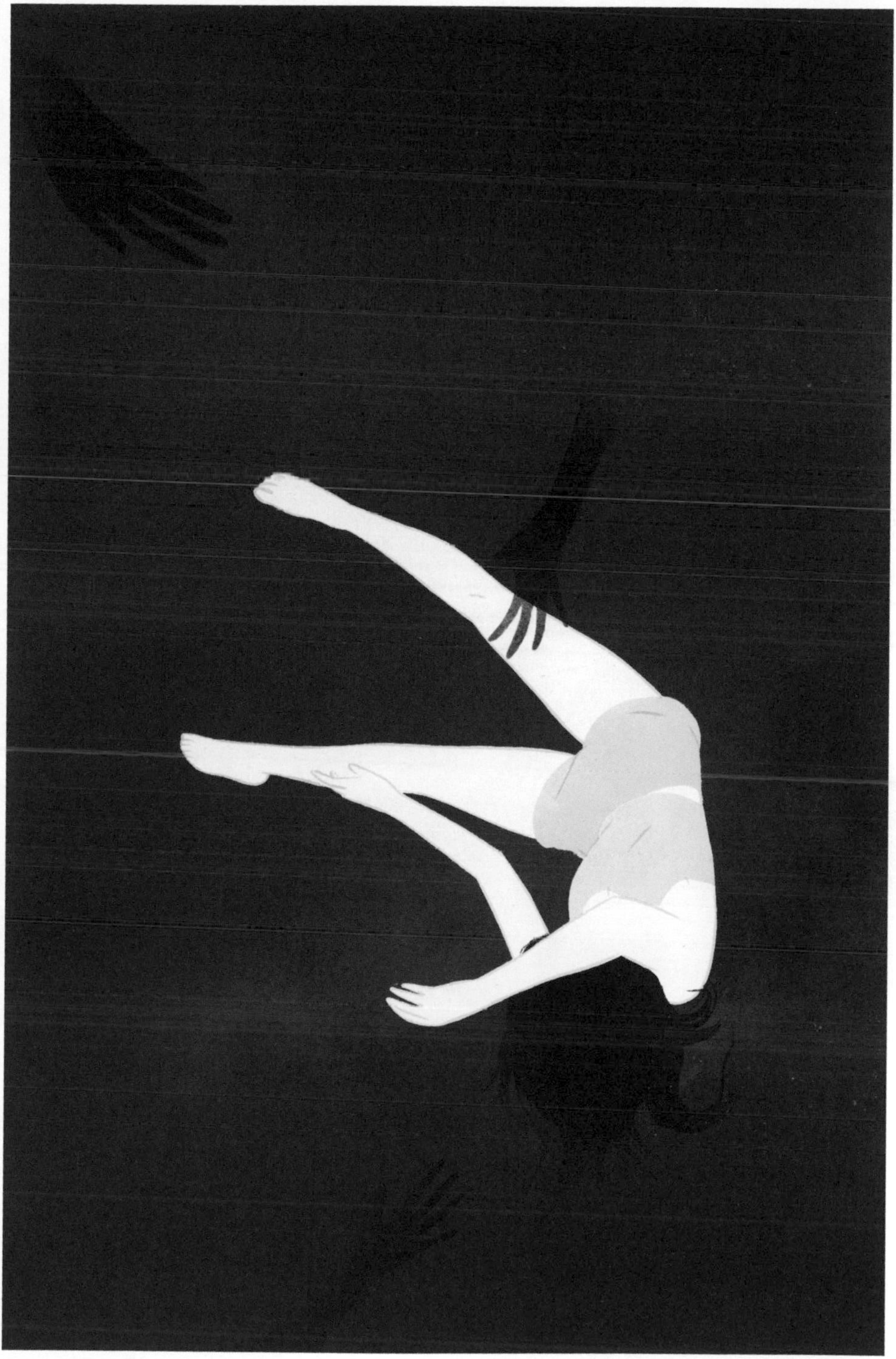

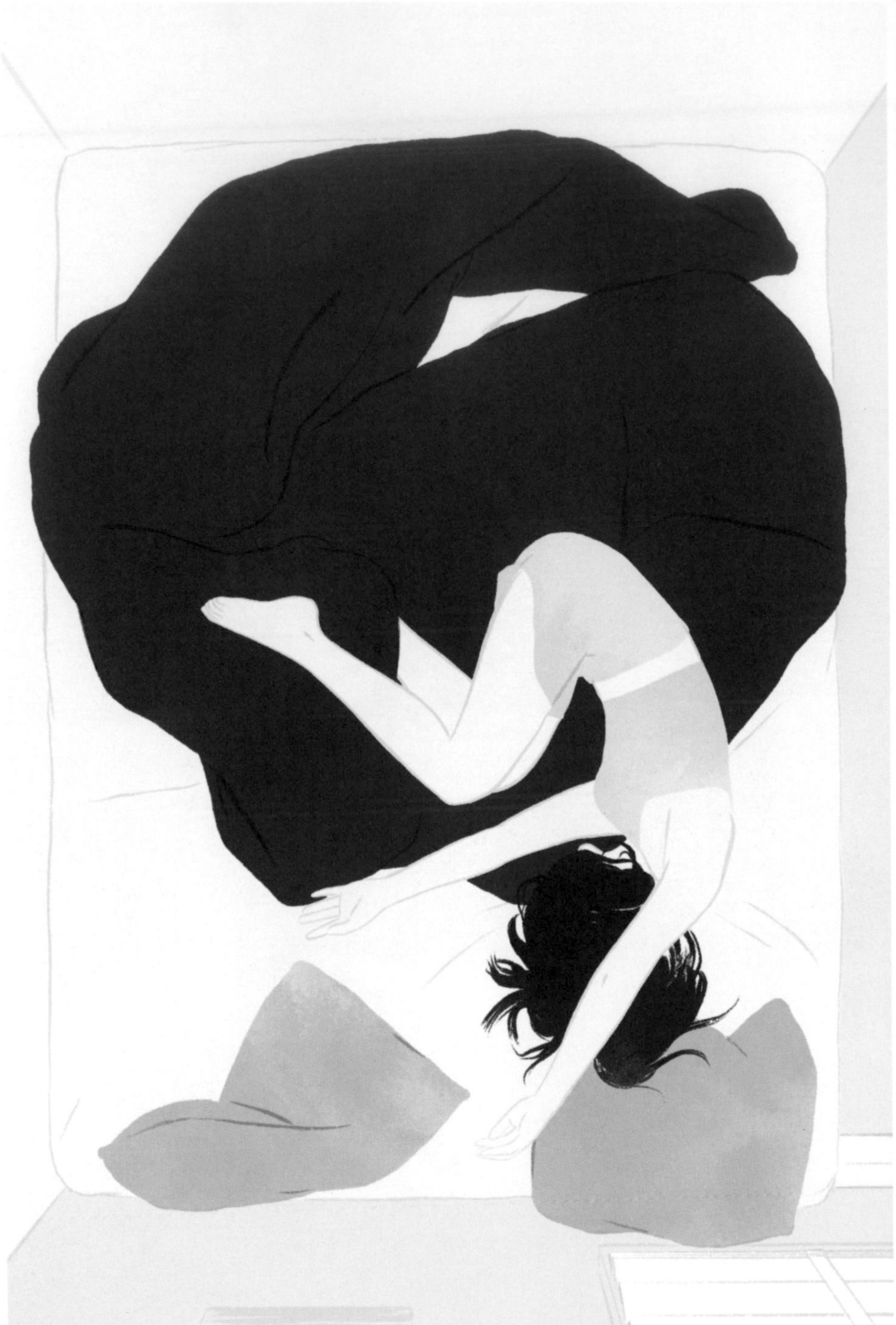

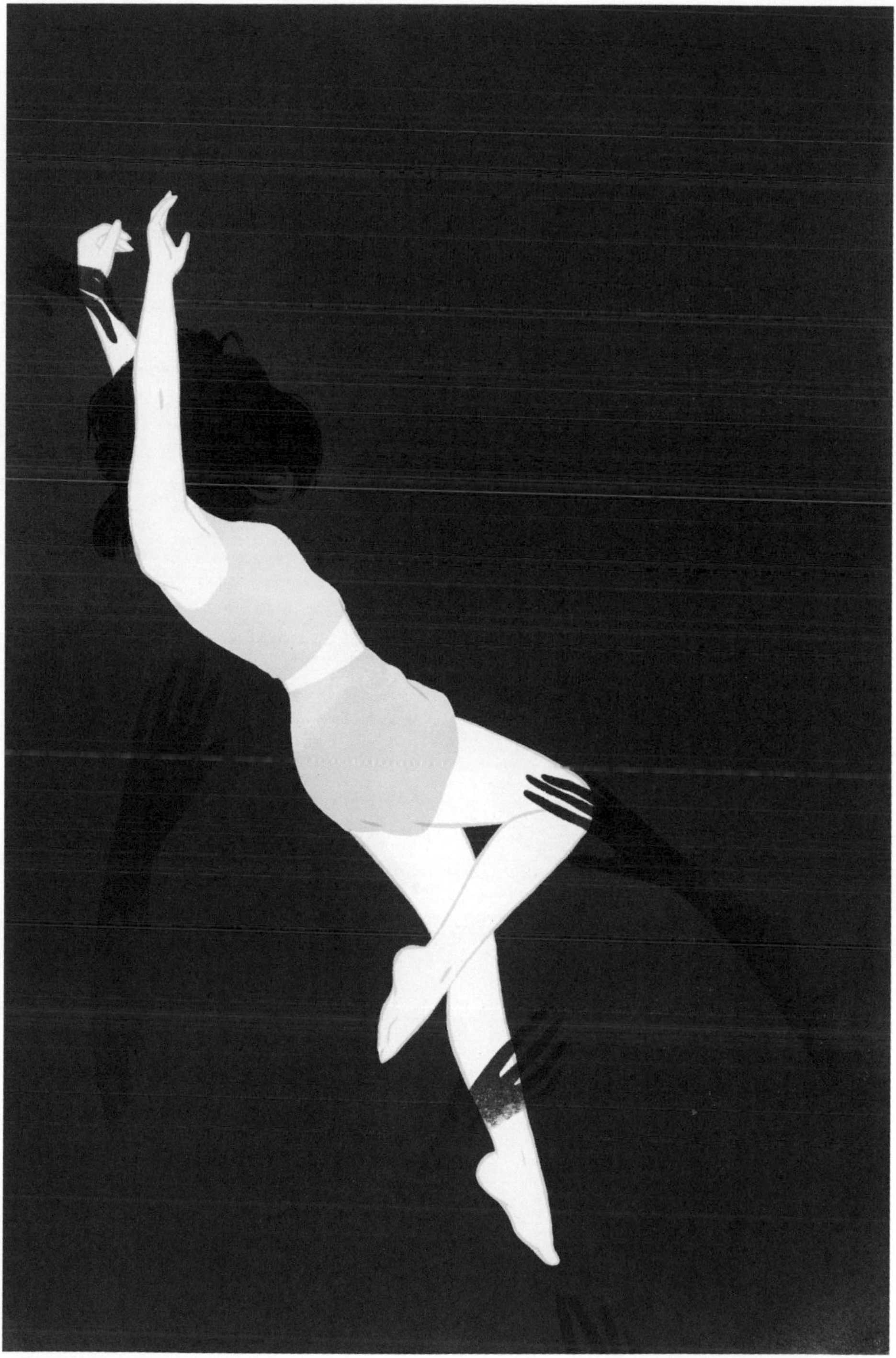

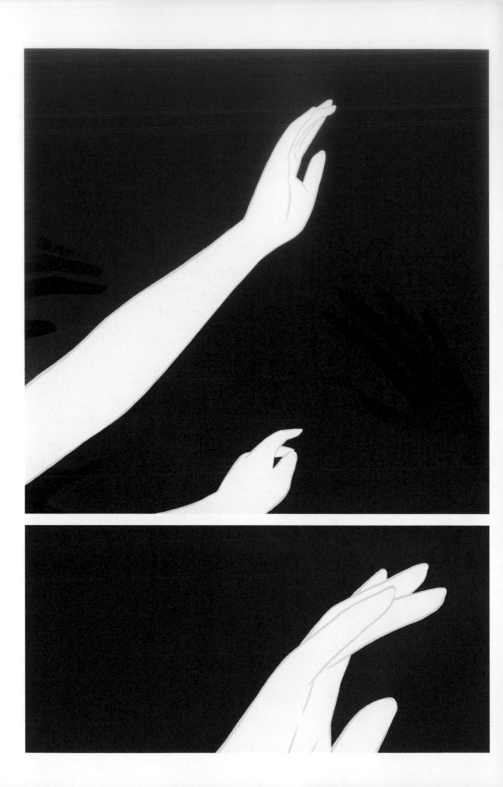

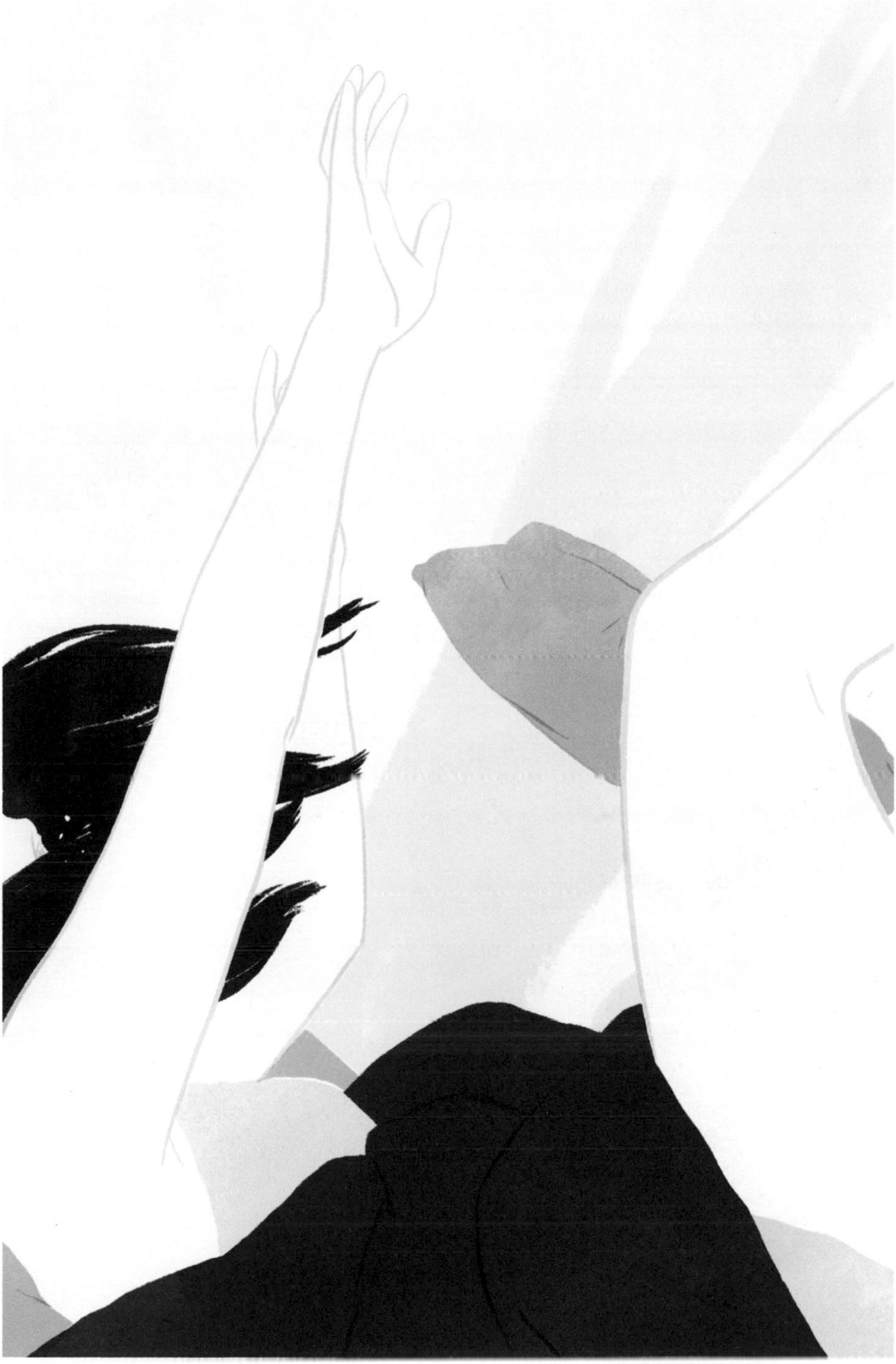

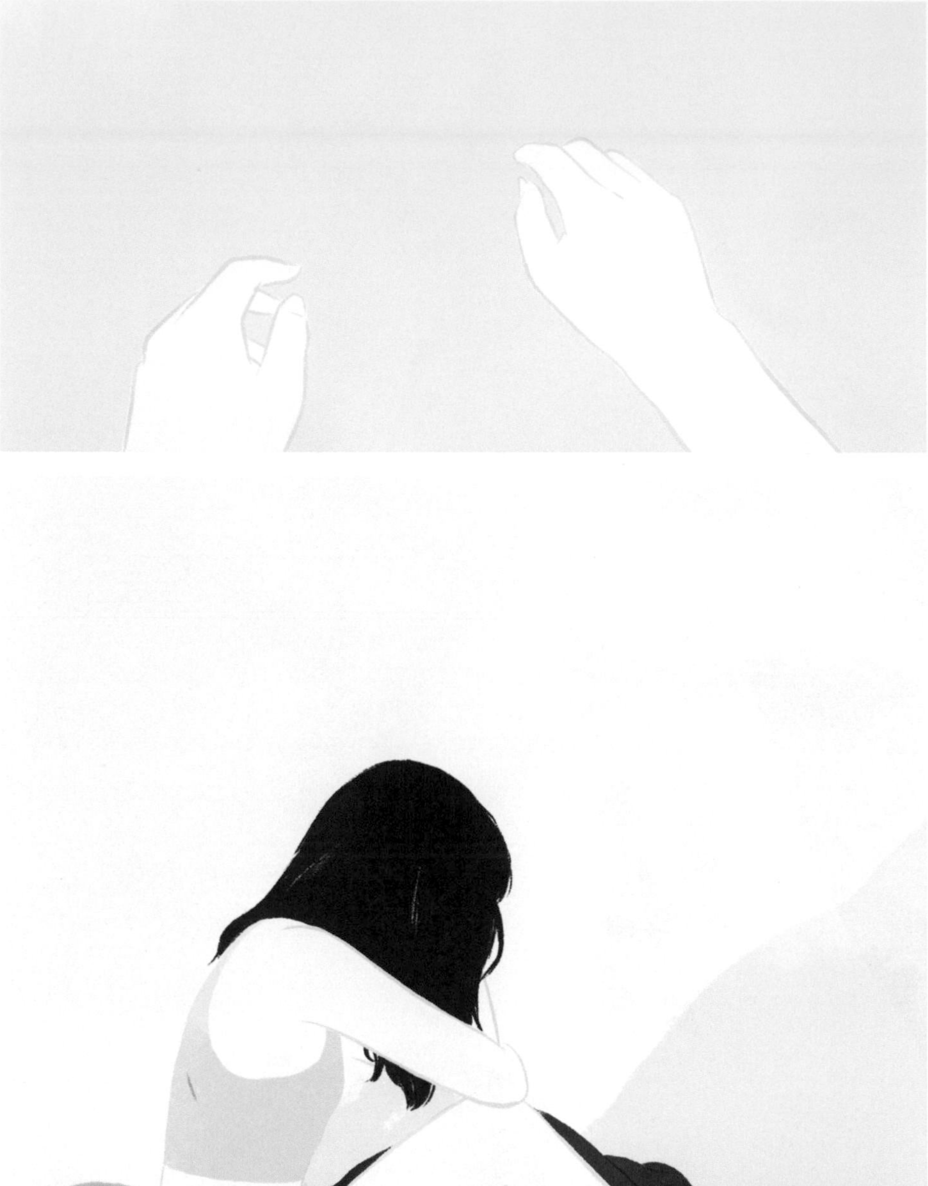

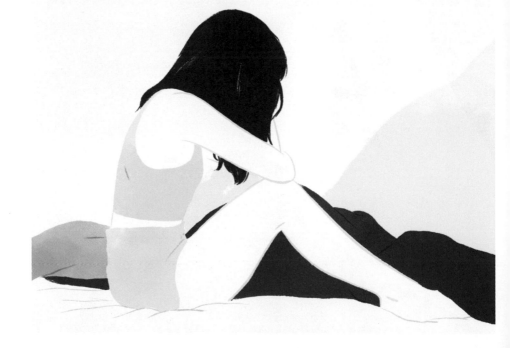

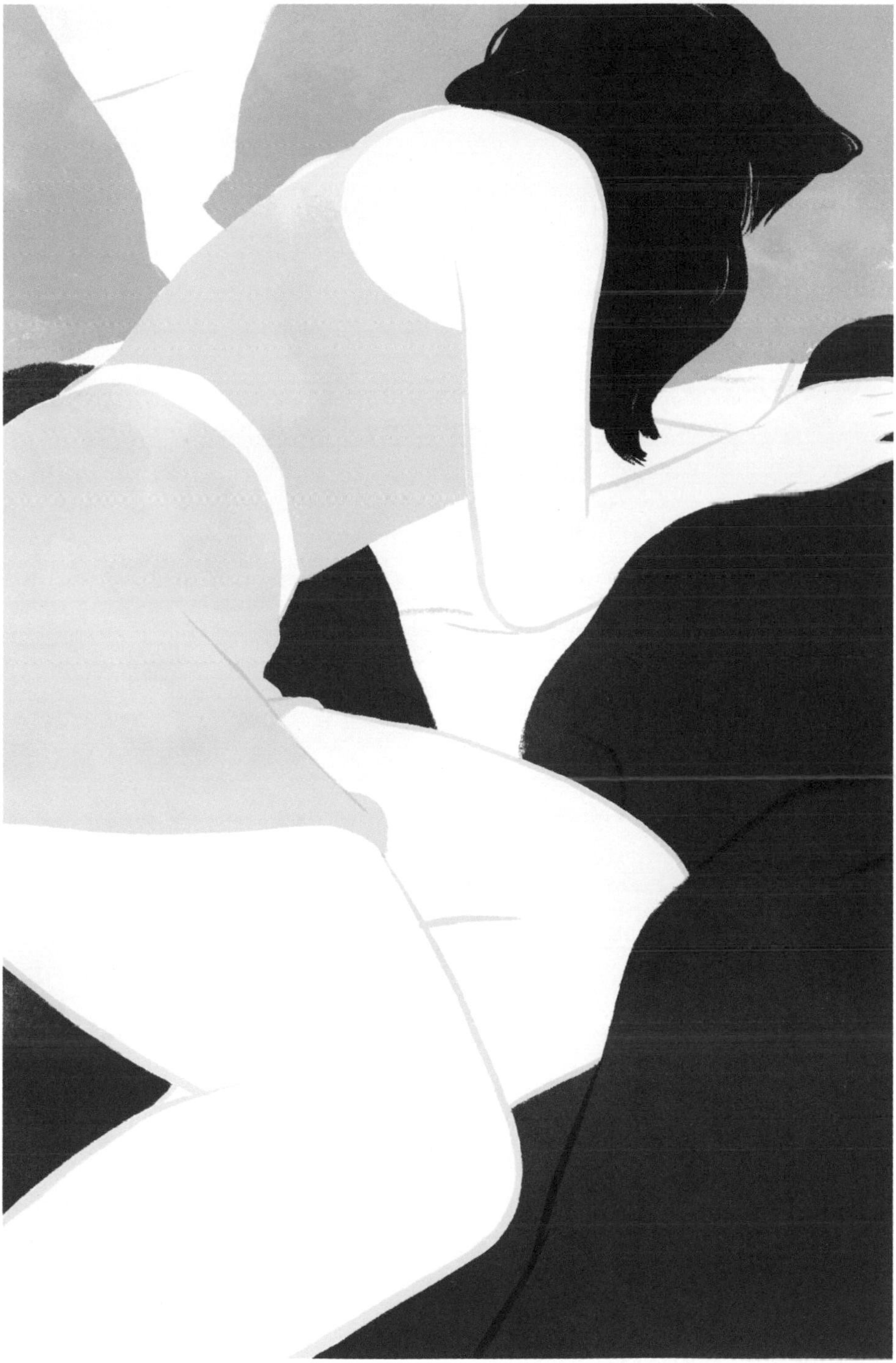

I don't want to eat

I don't want to sleep

I don't want to live

I don't want to die

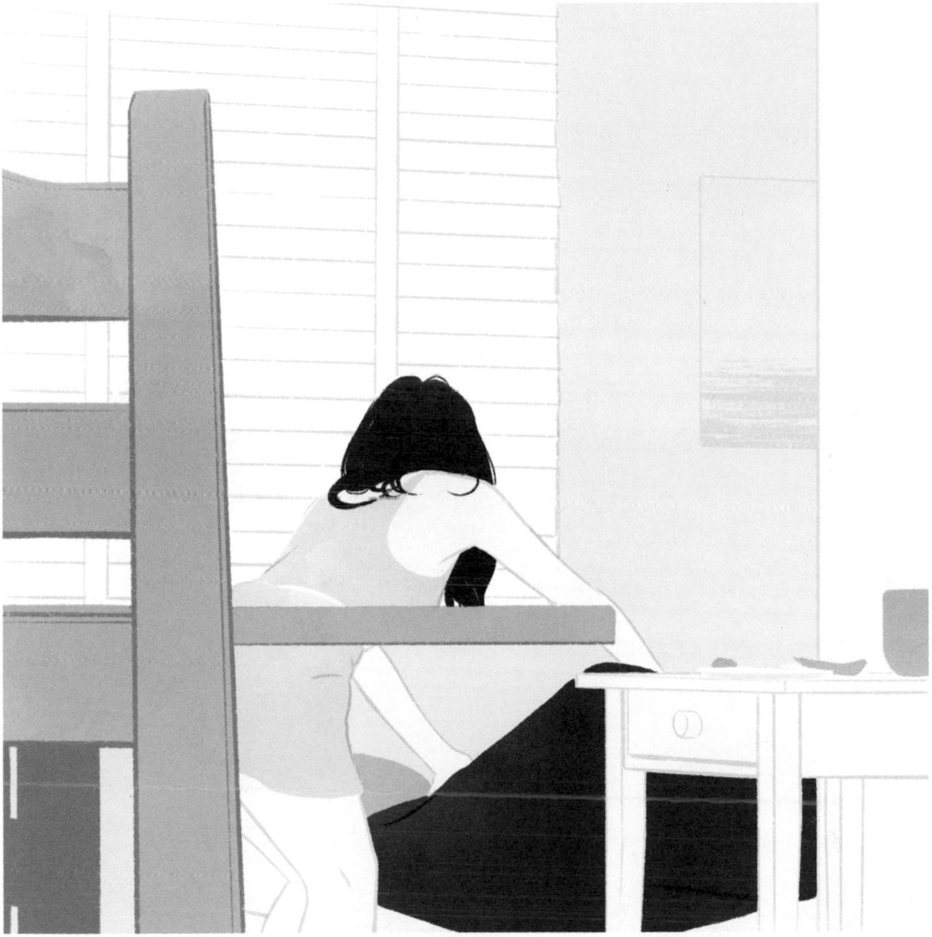

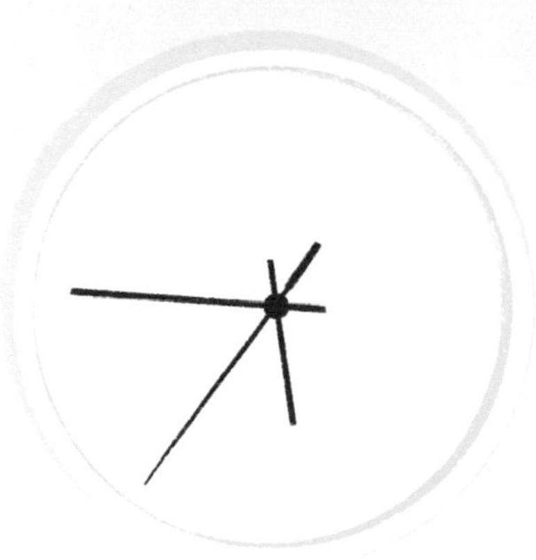

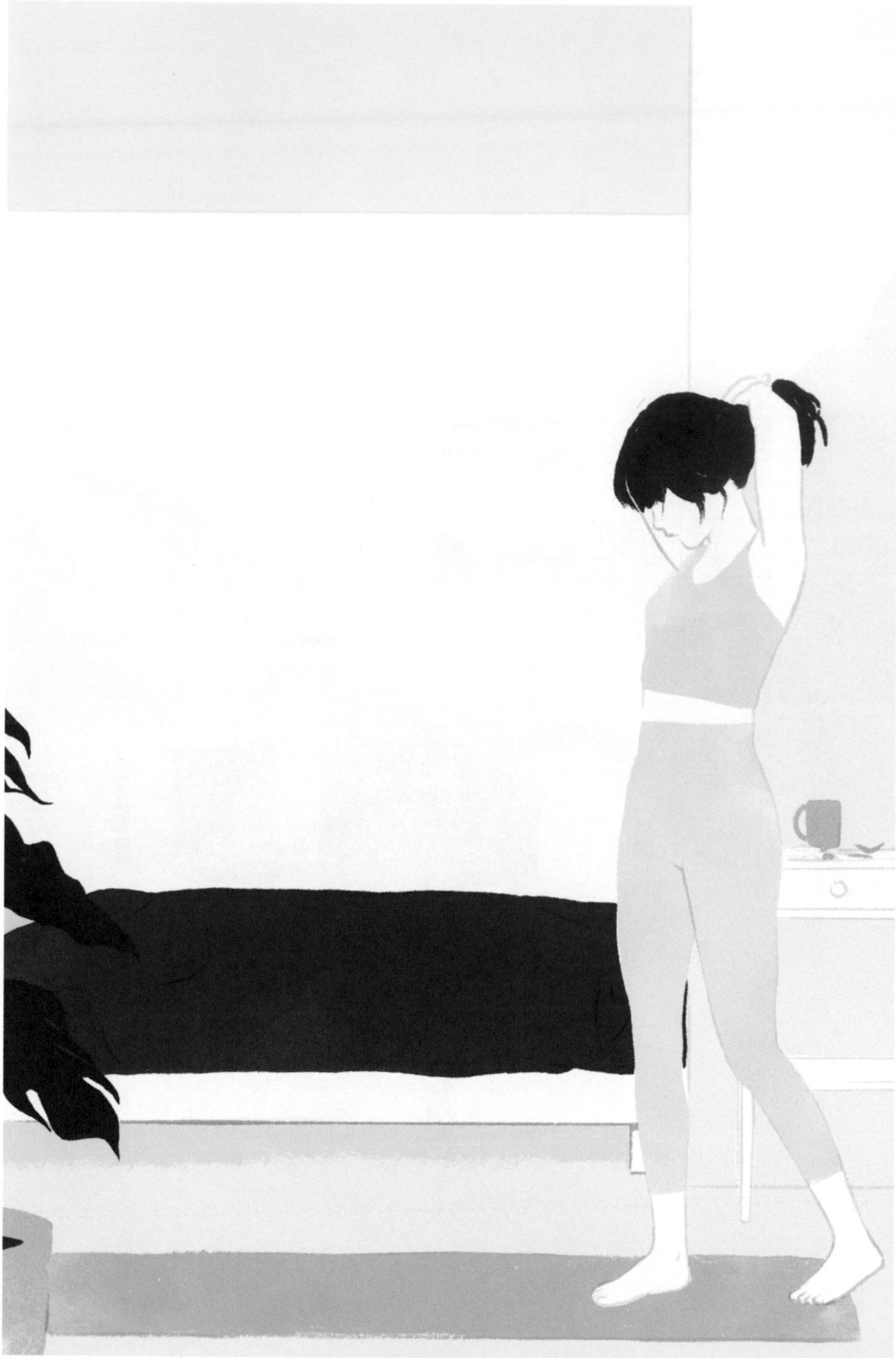

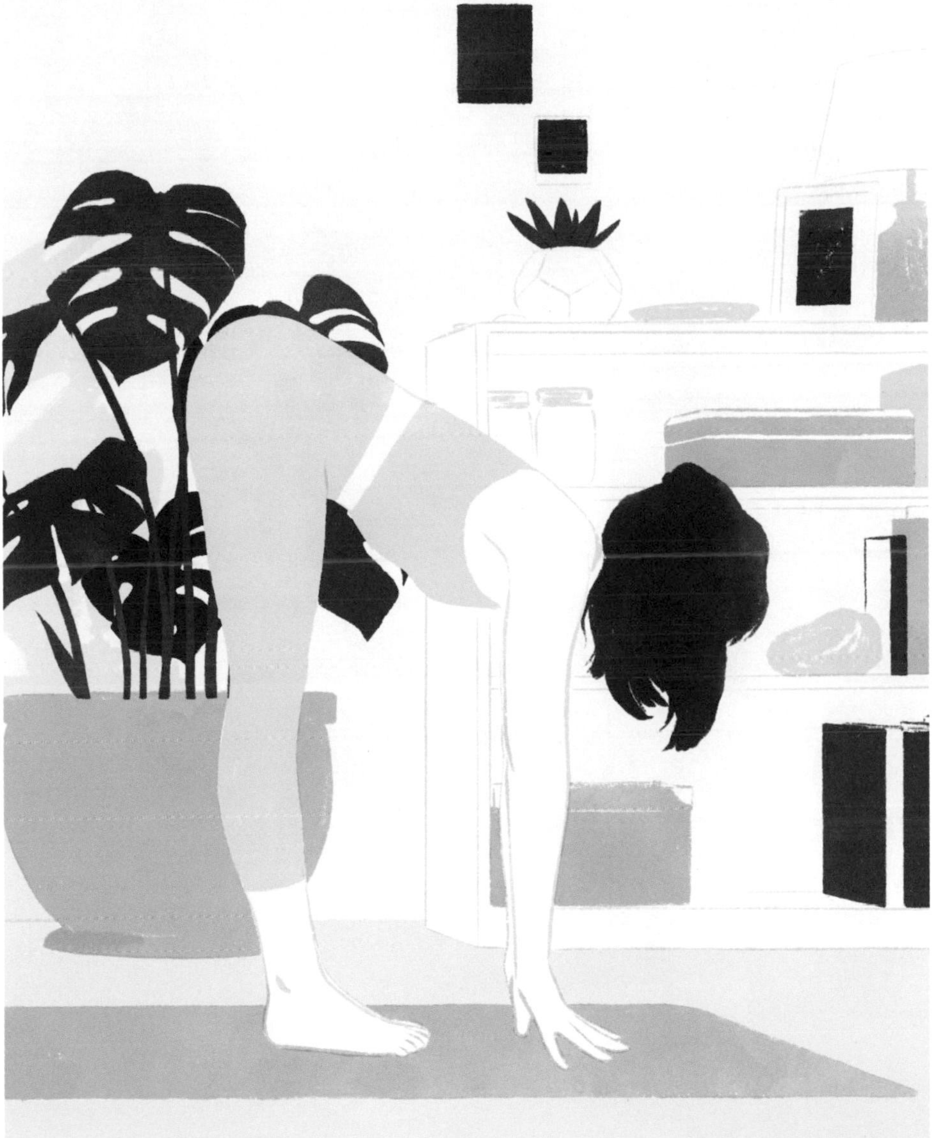

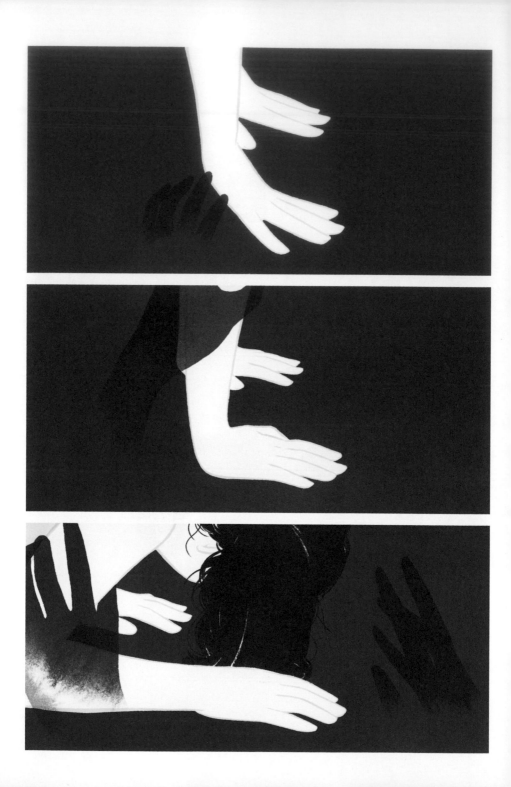

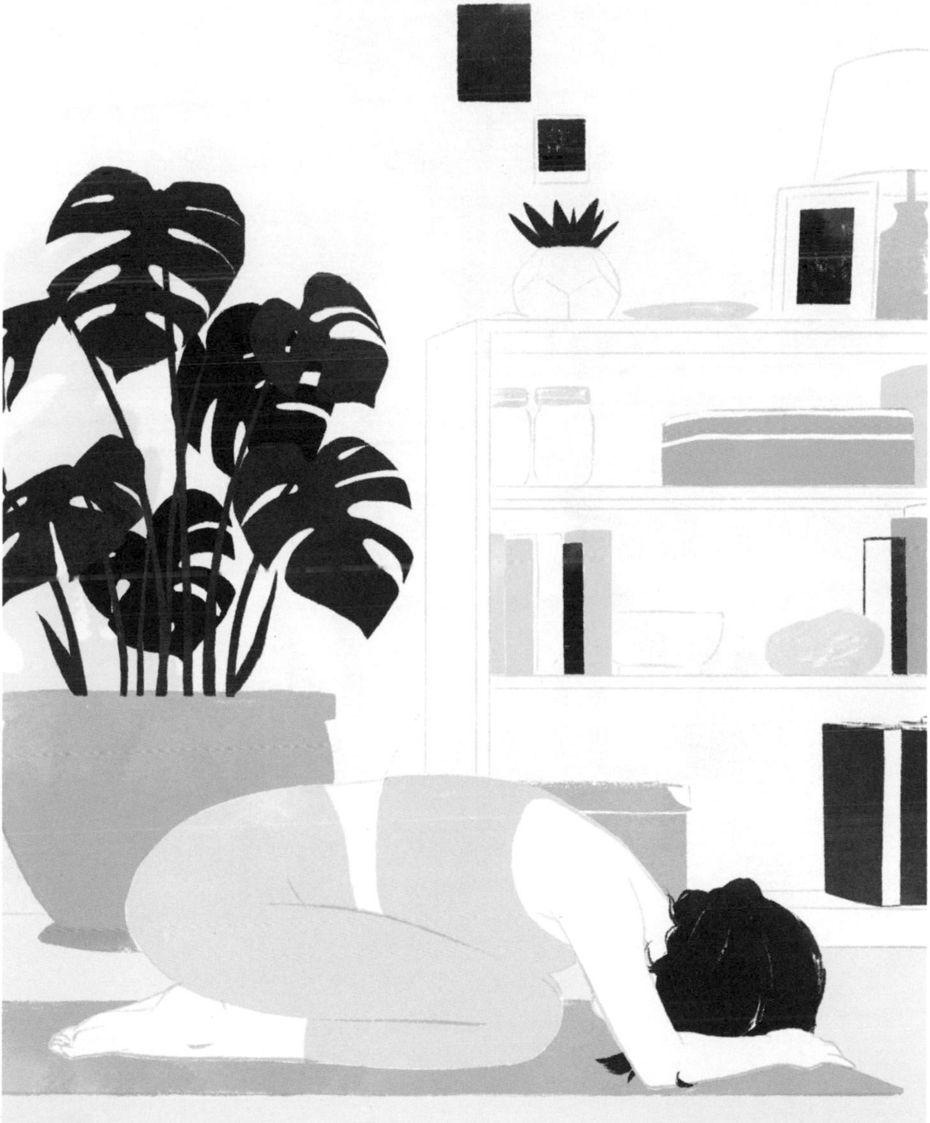

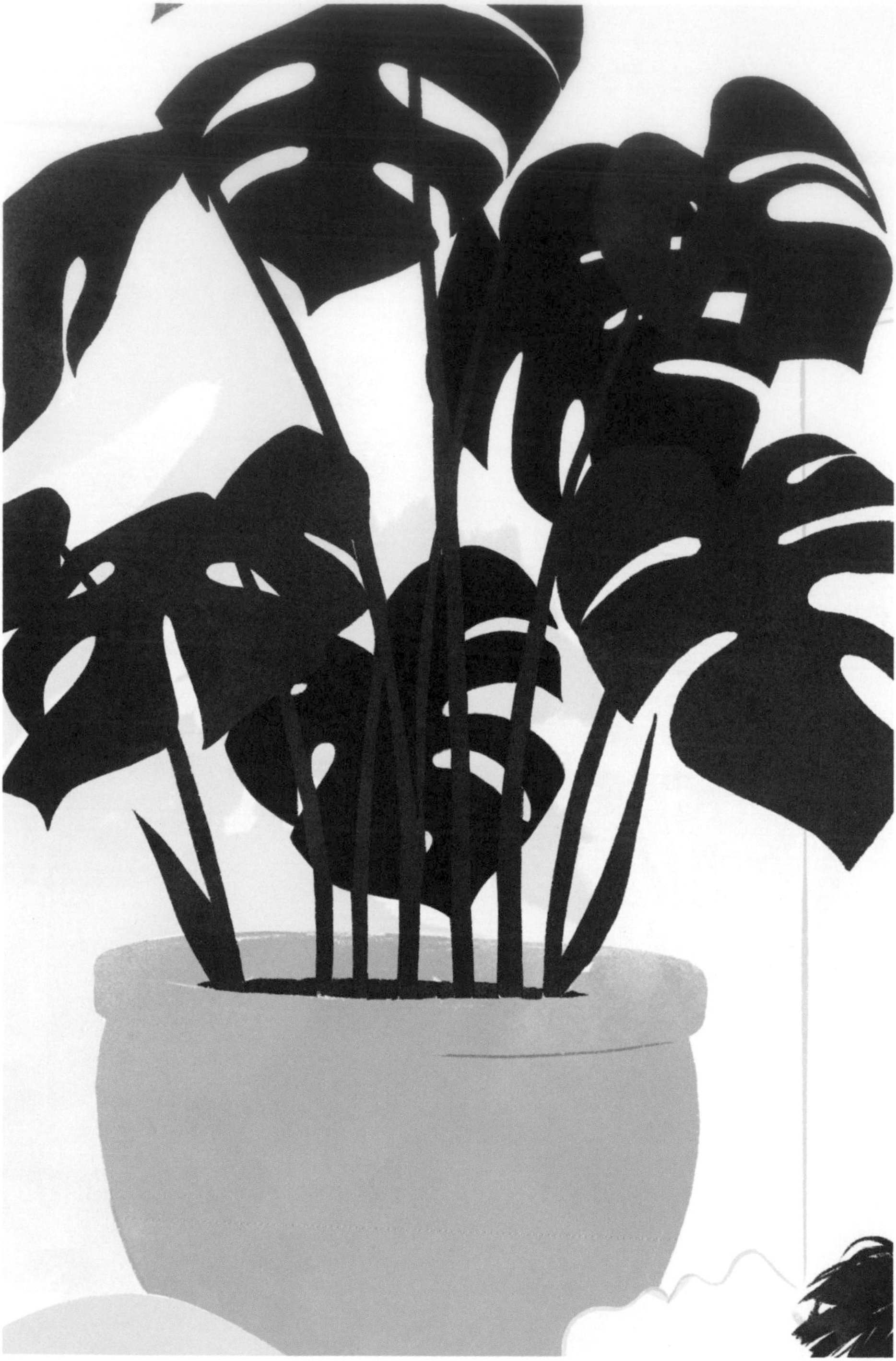

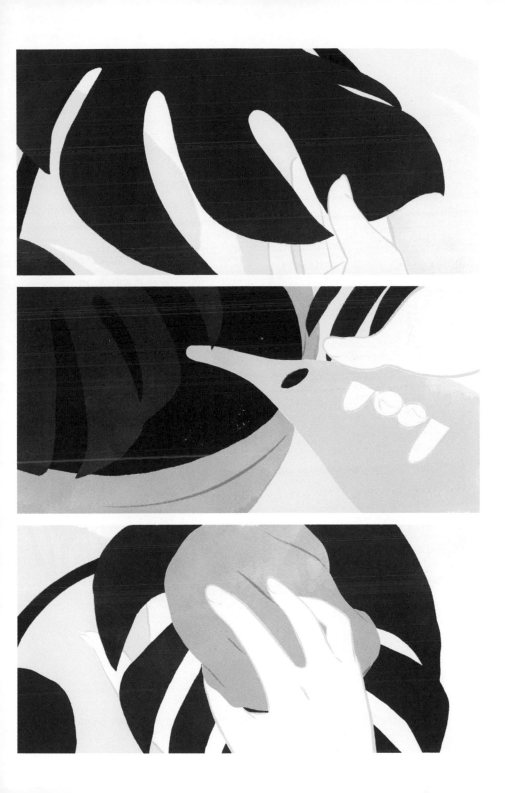

I don't want to laugh

I don't want to cry

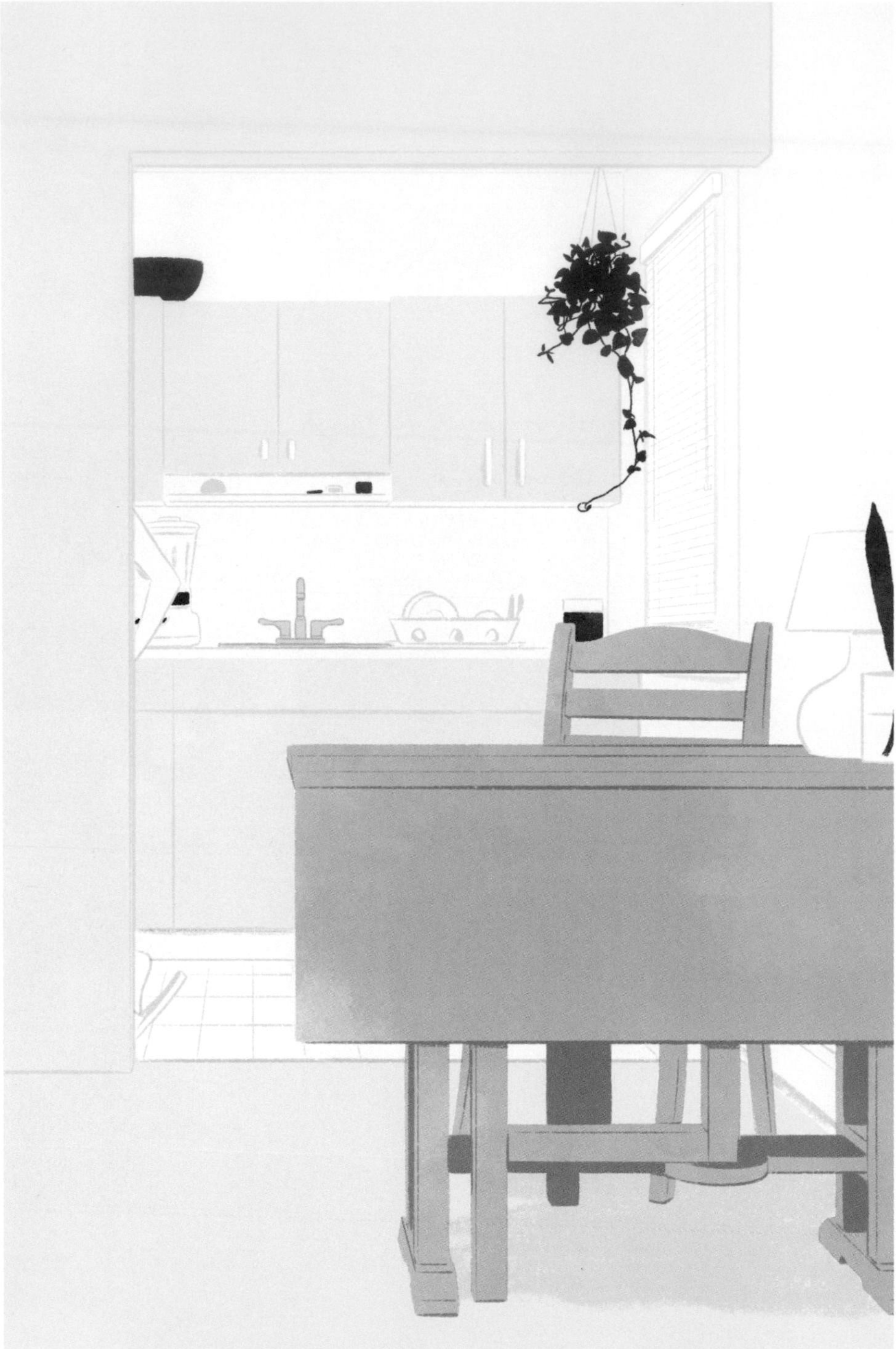

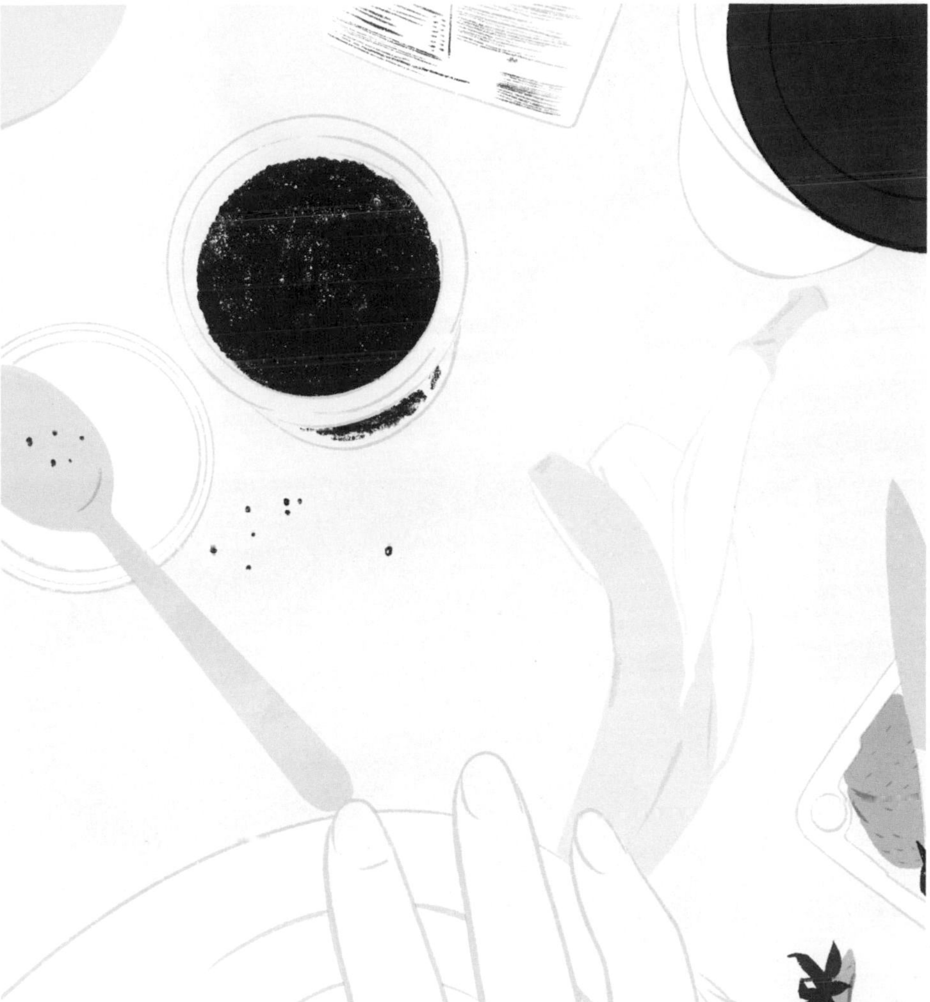

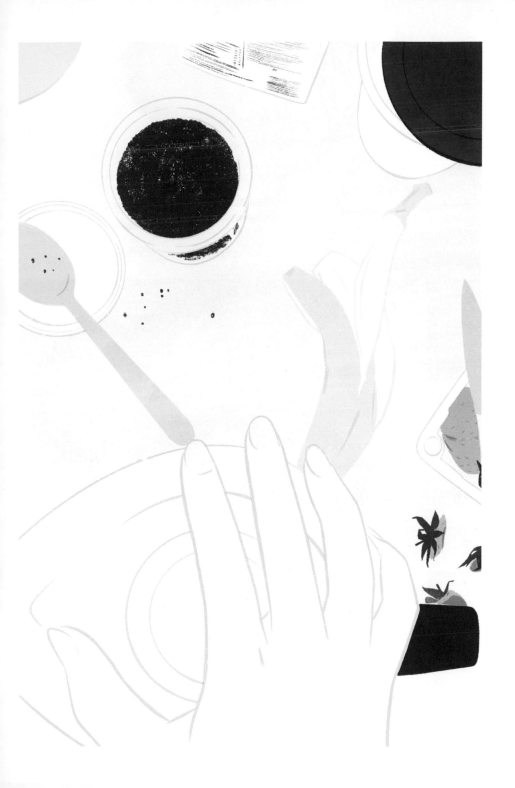

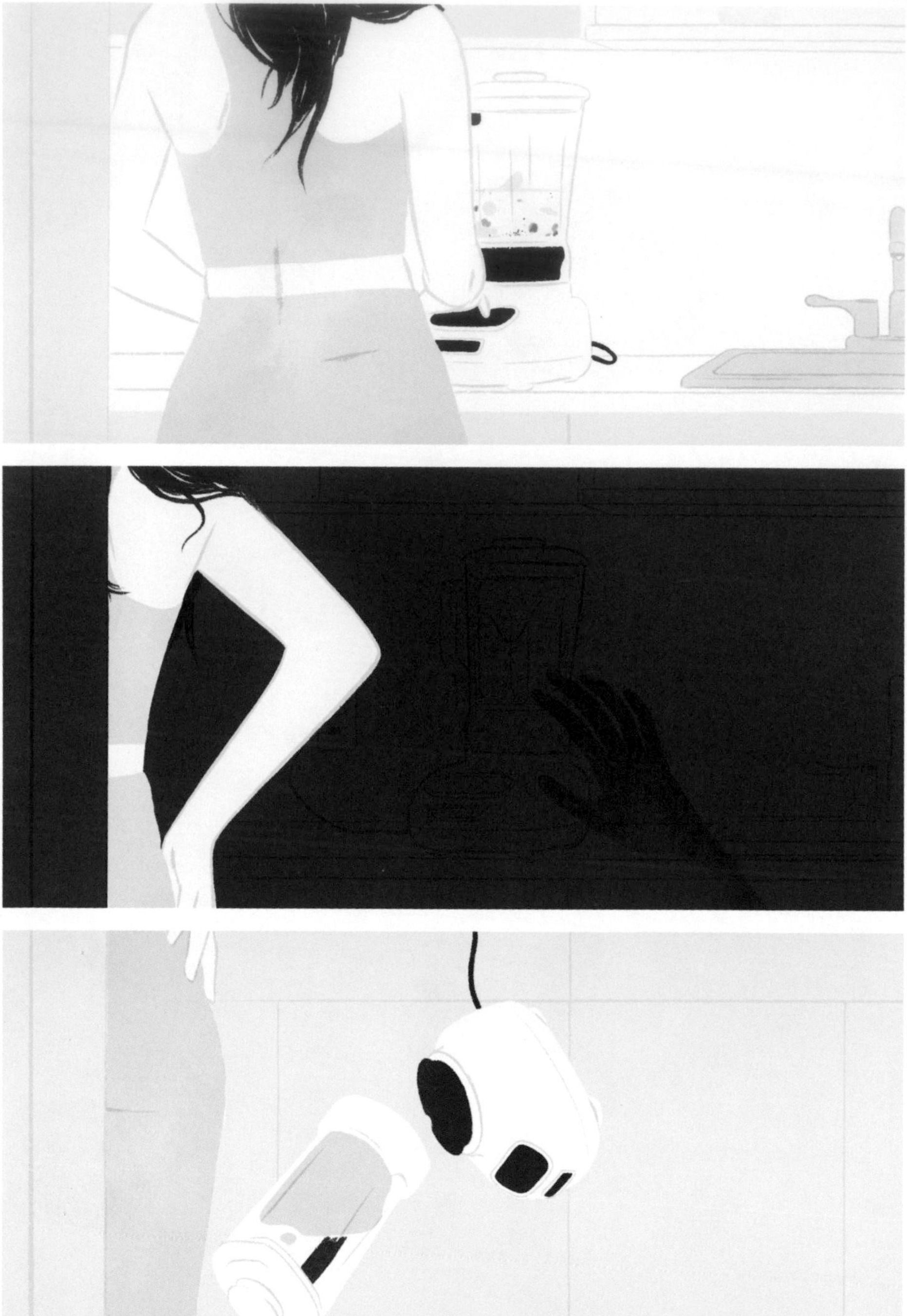

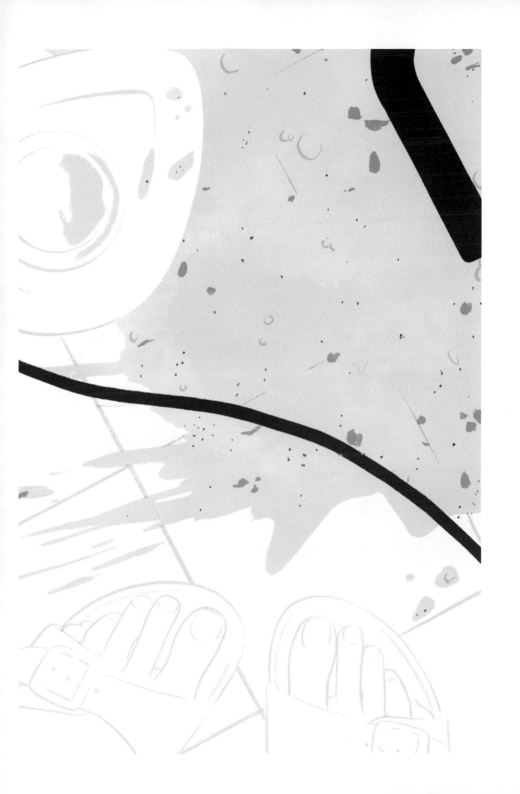

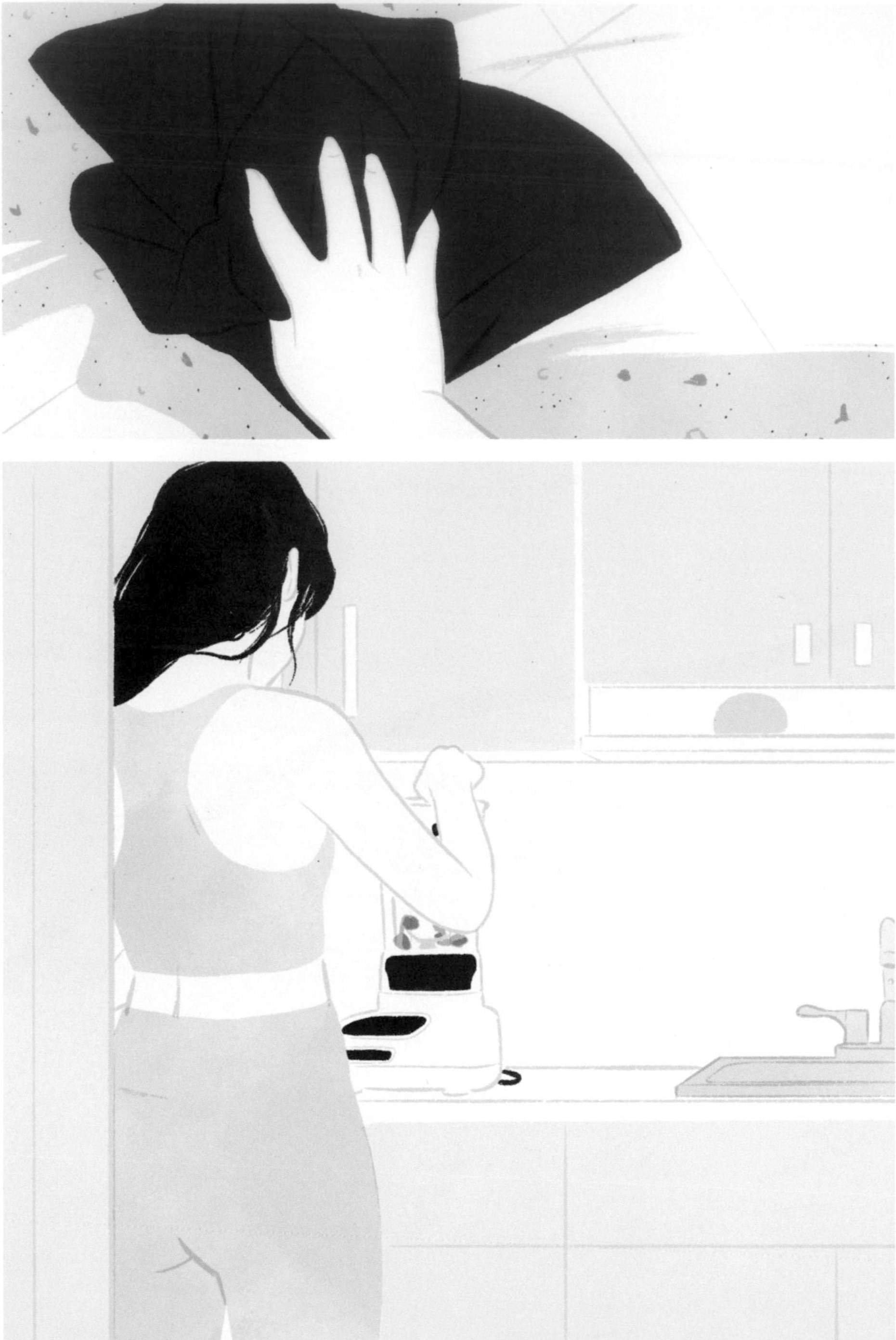

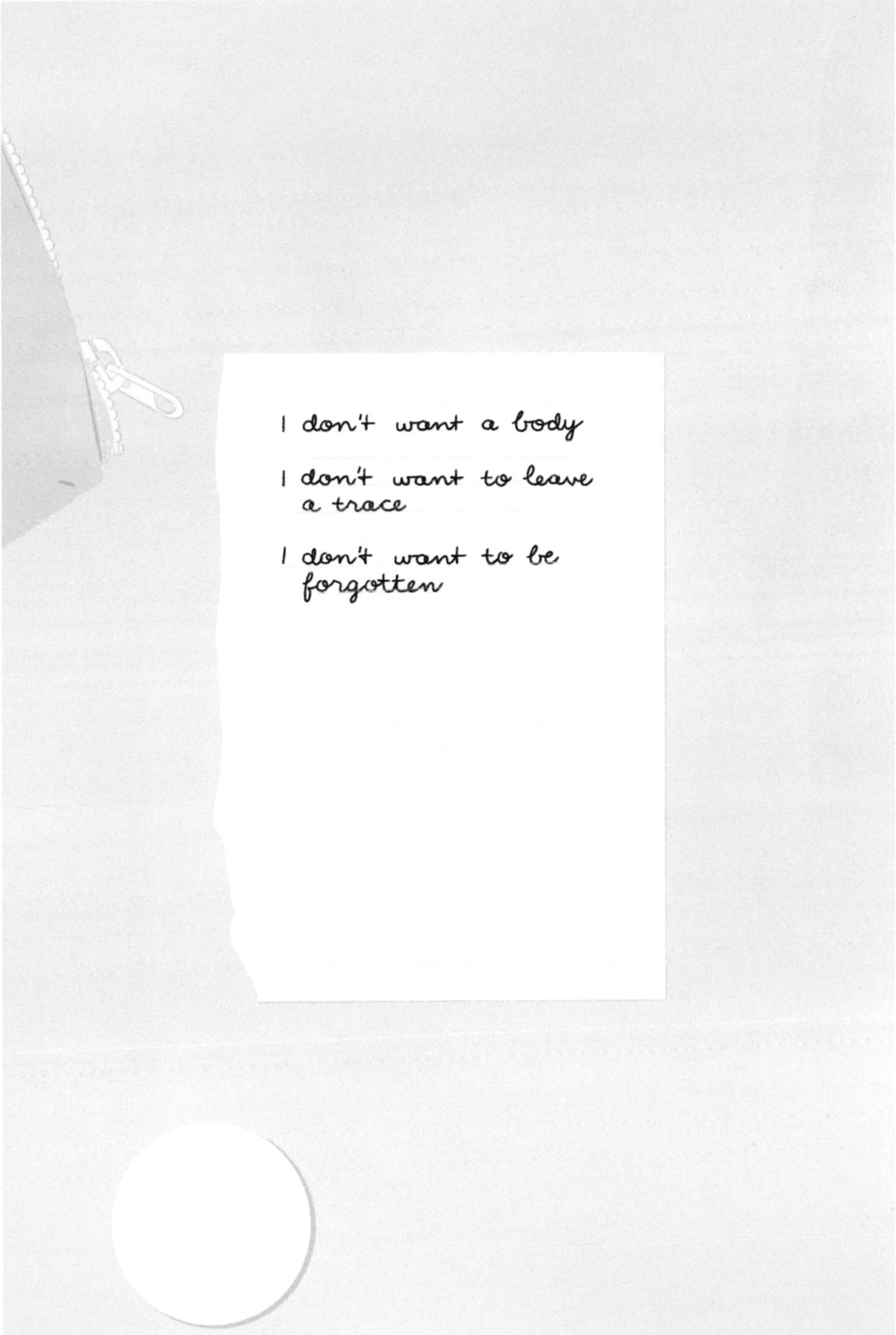
I don't want a body
I don't want to leave a trace
I don't want to be forgotten

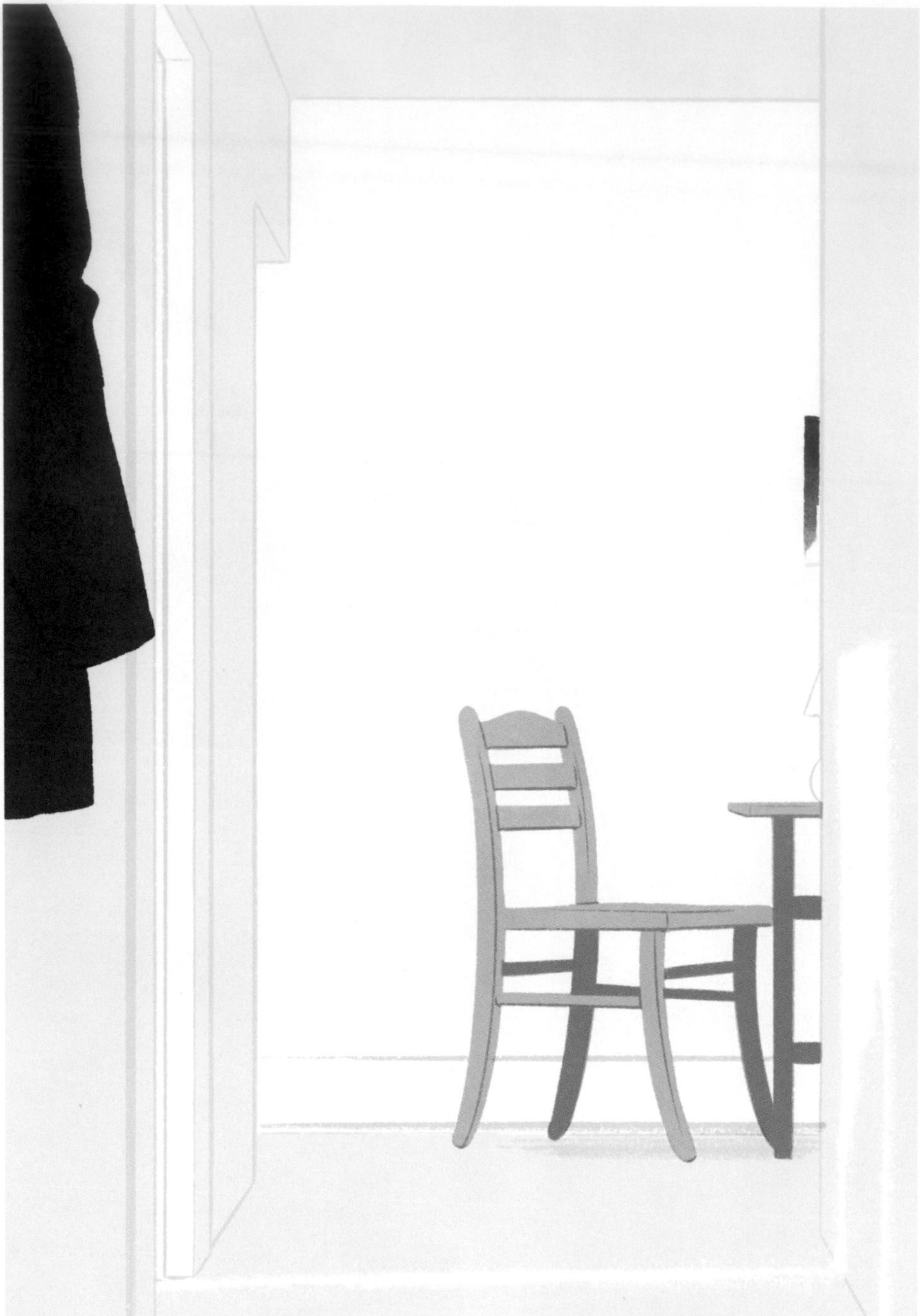

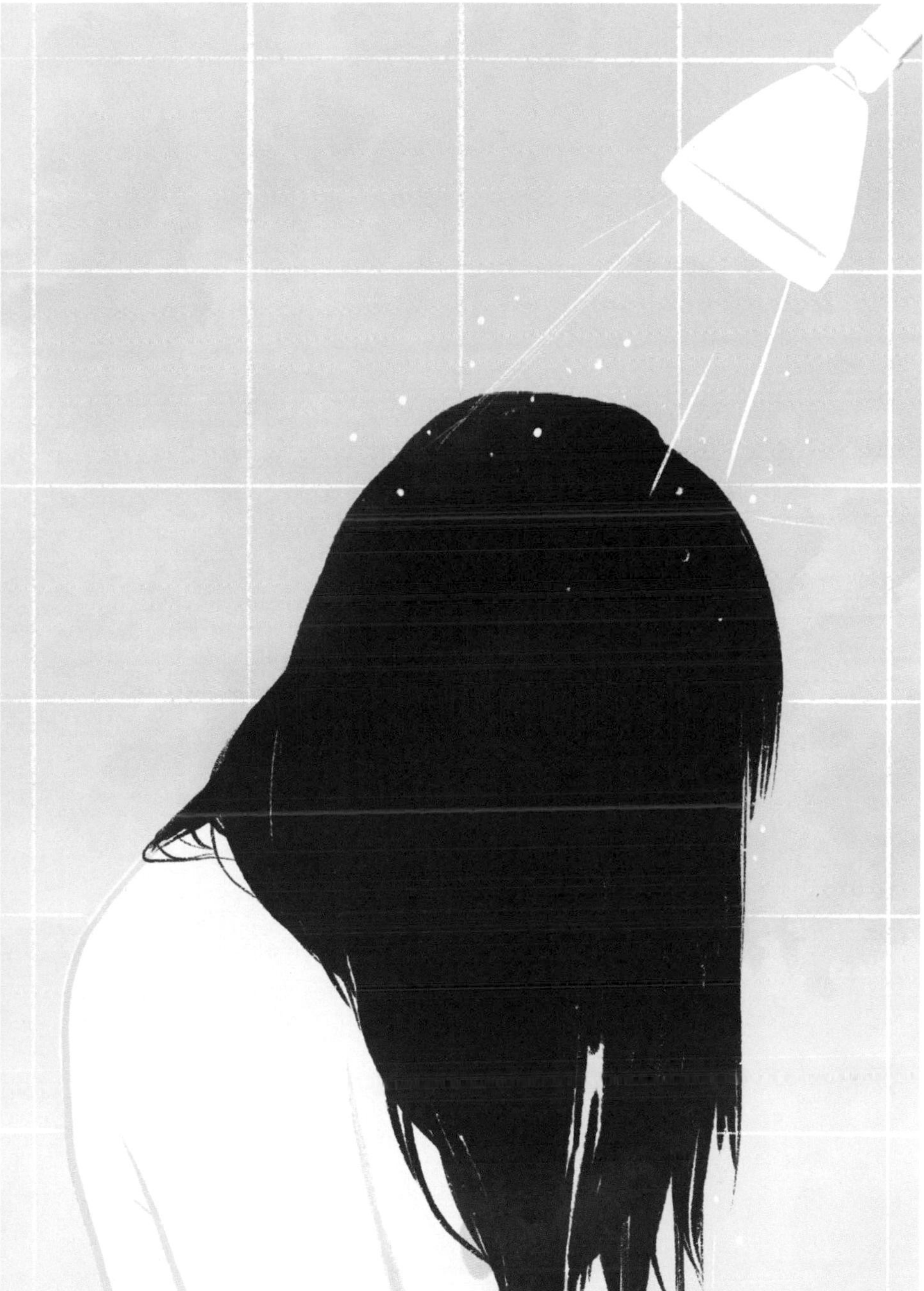

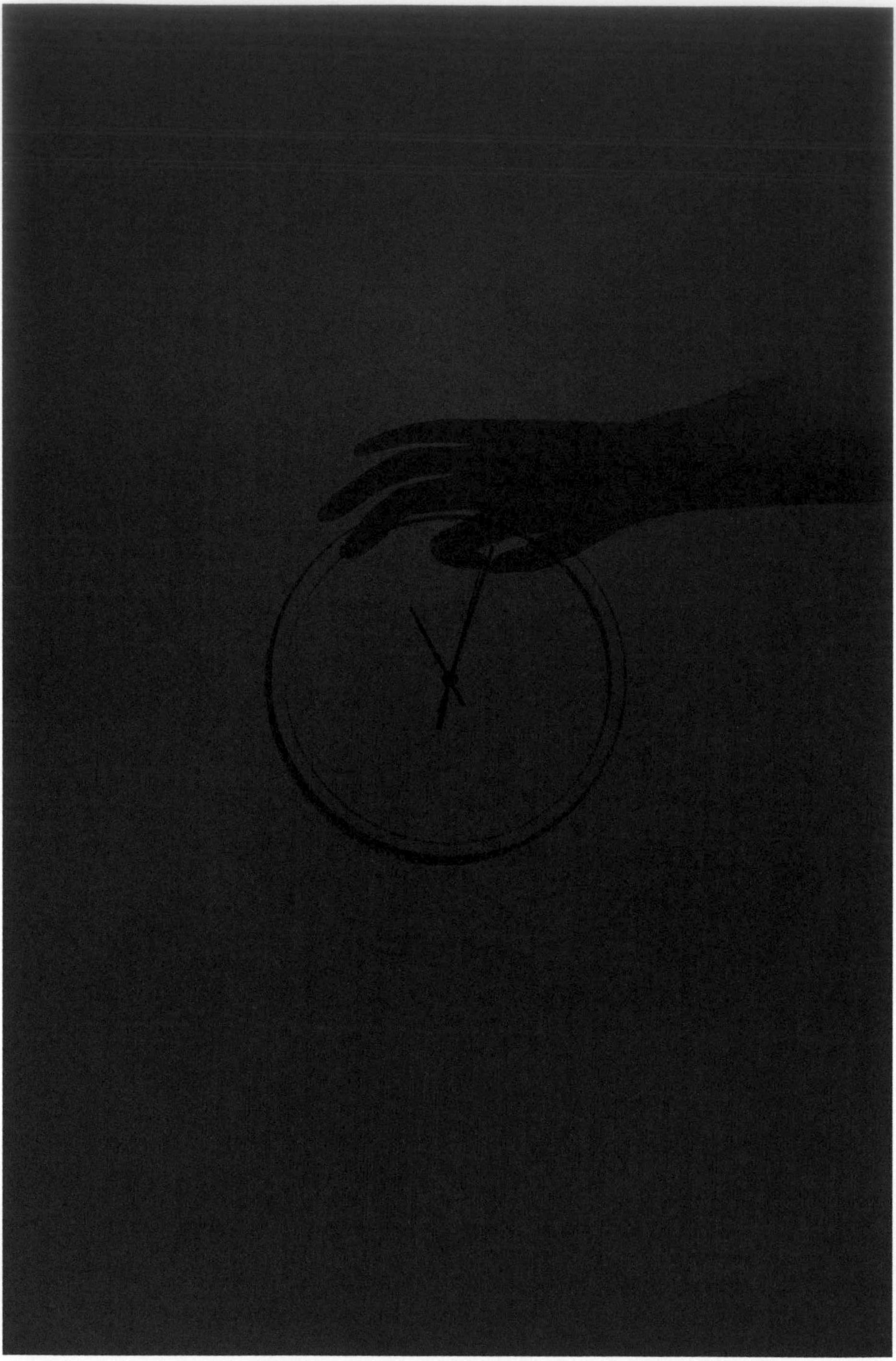

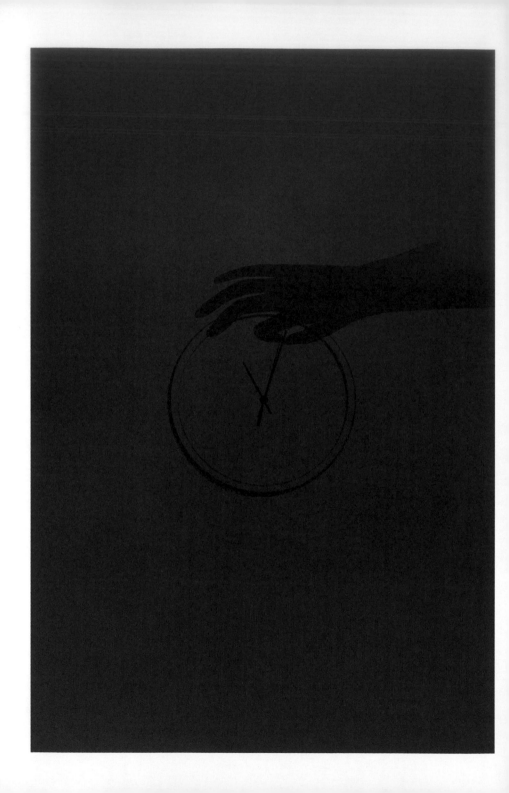

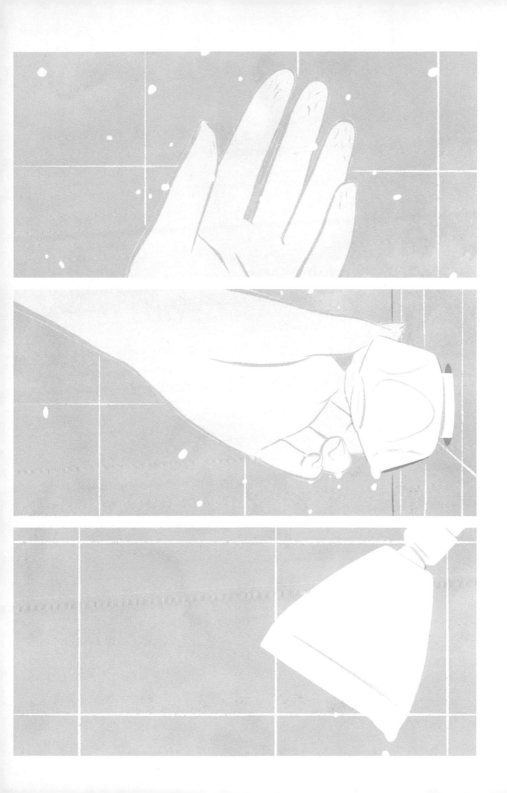

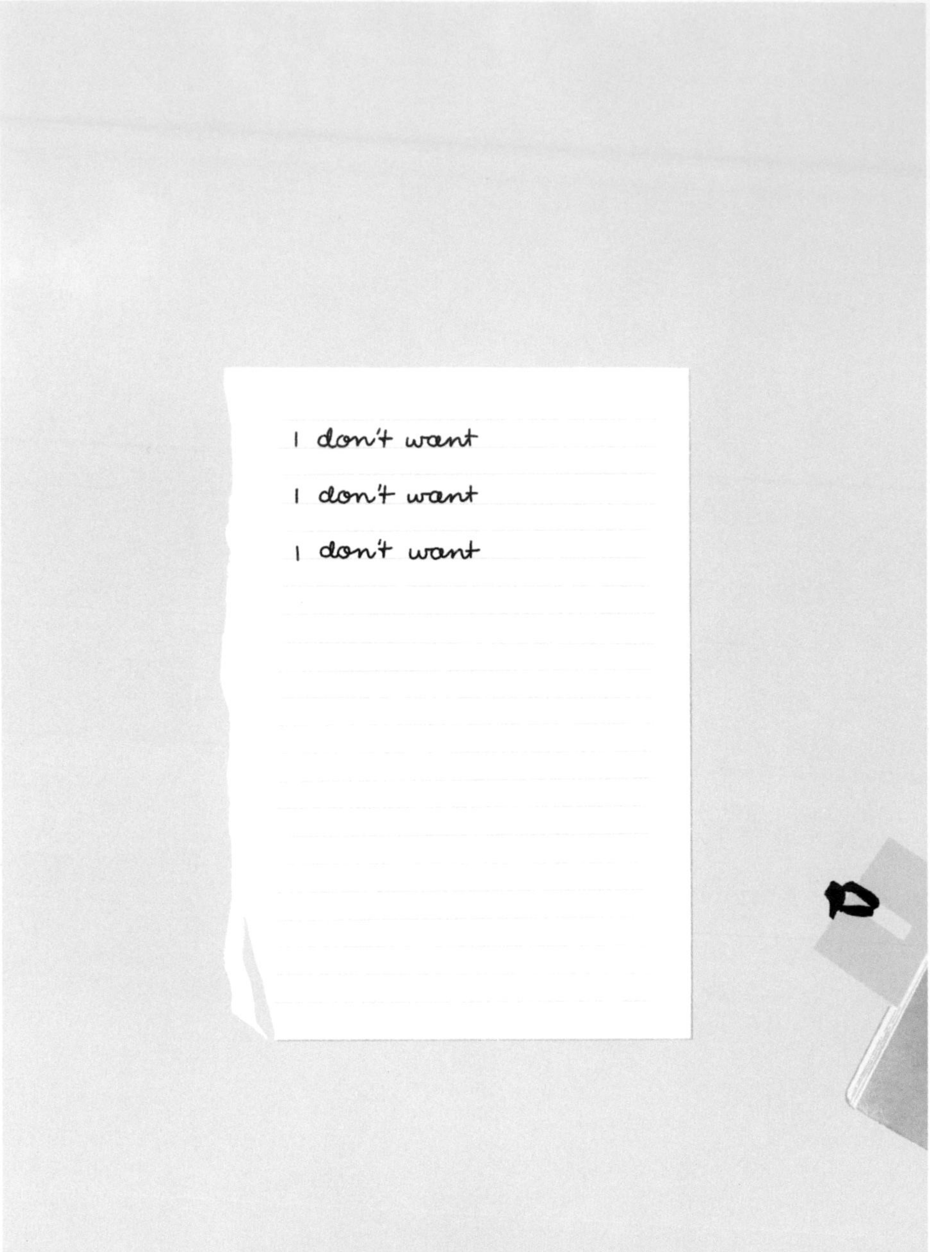
I don't want
I don't want
I don't want

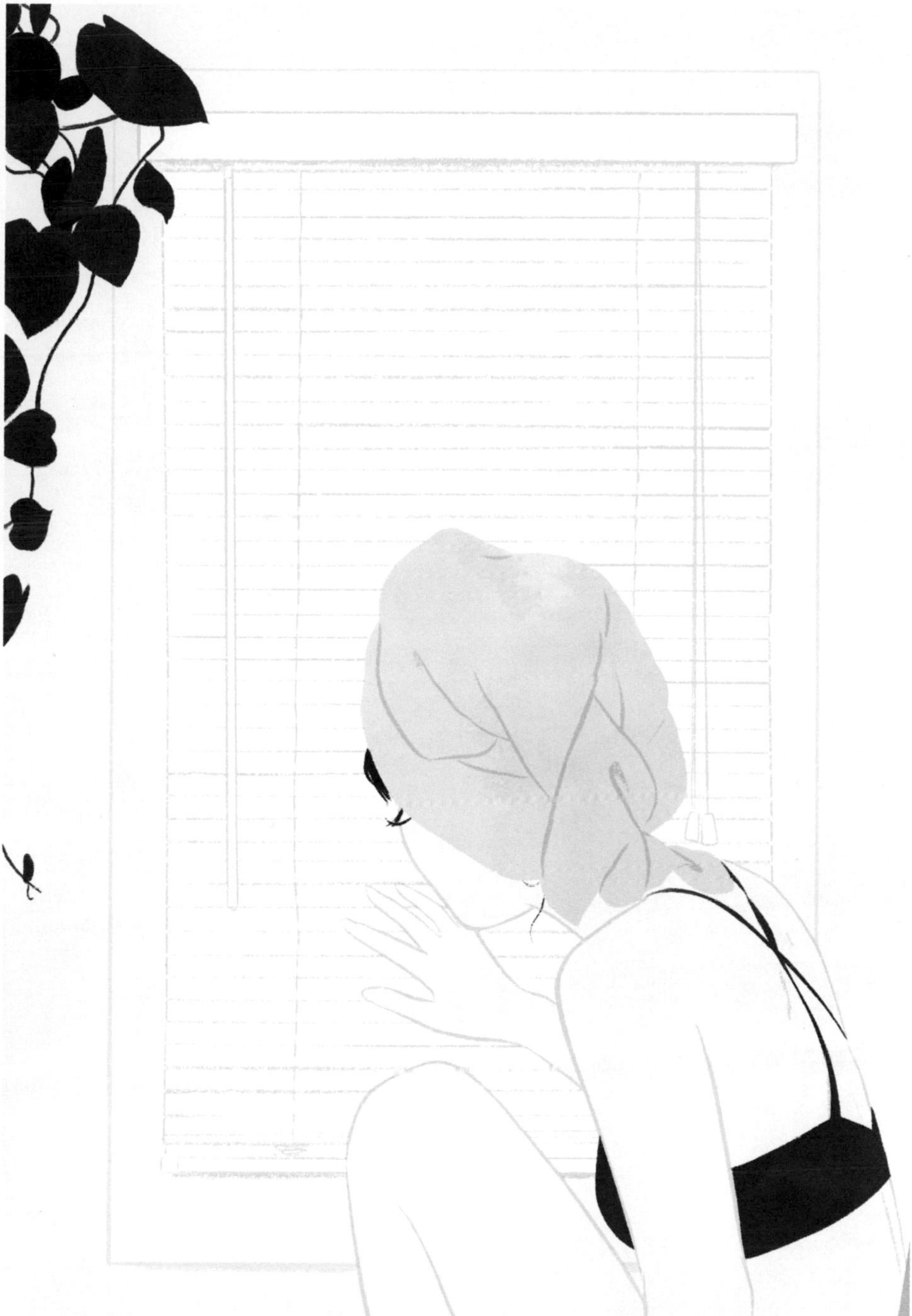

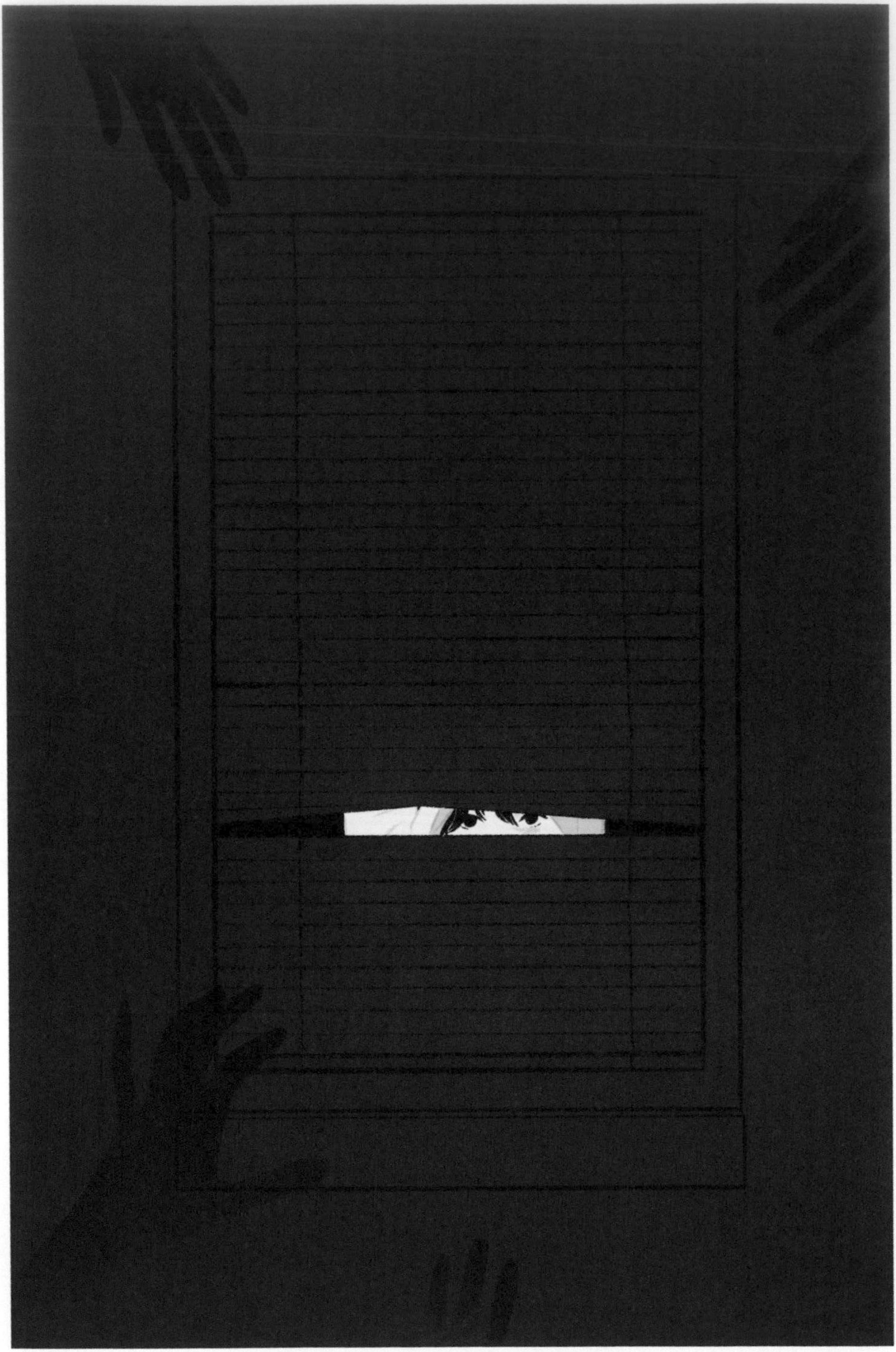

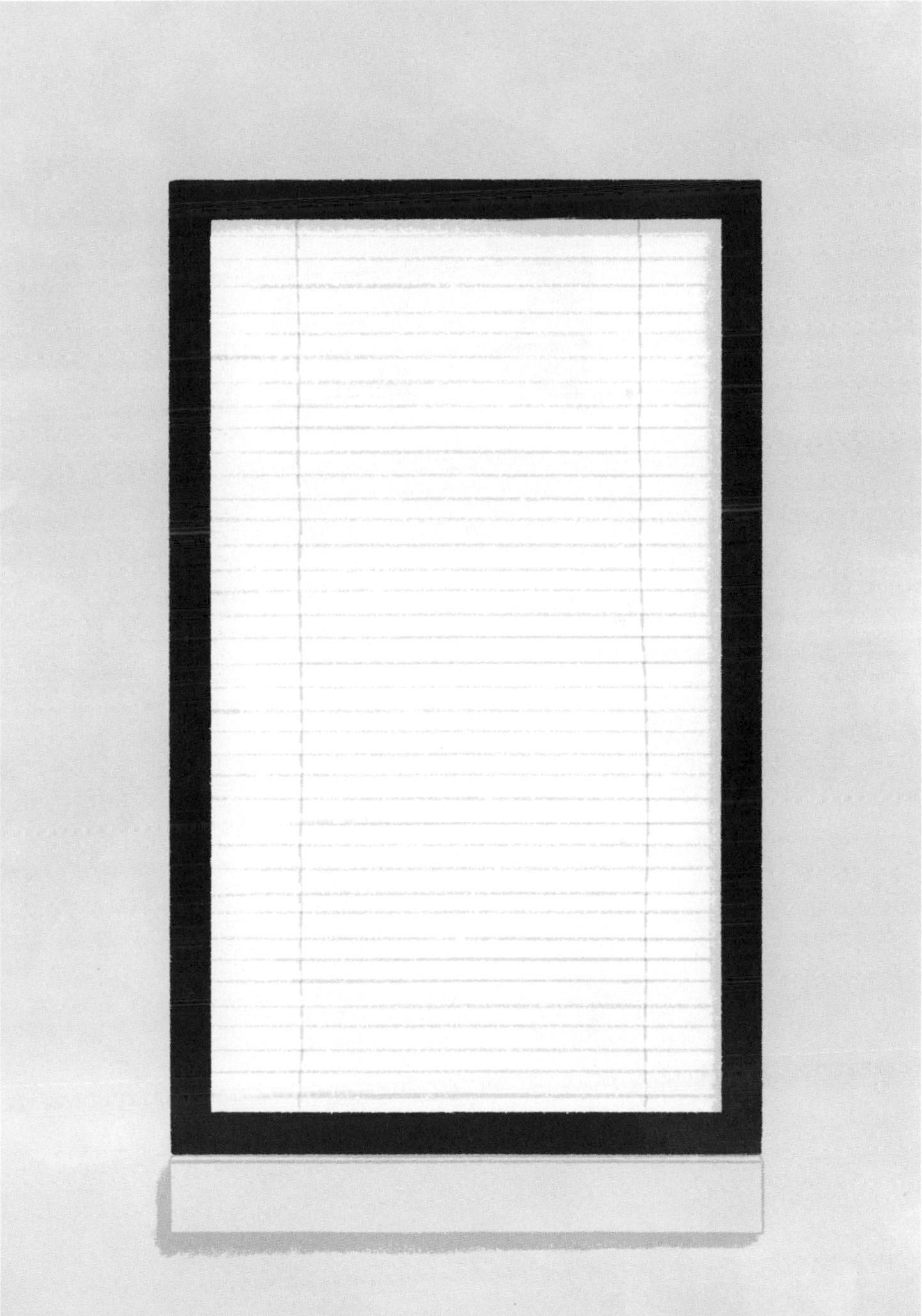

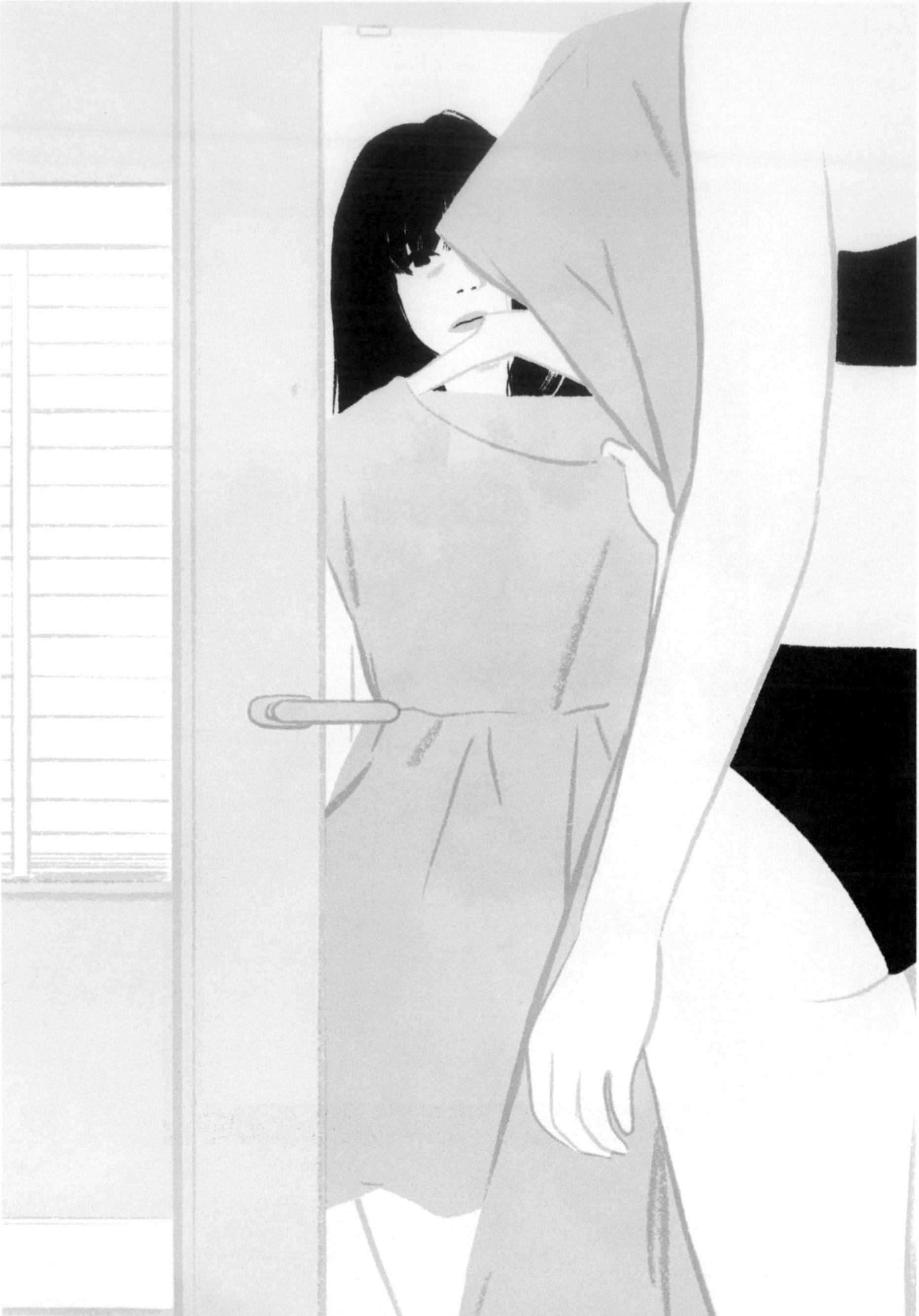

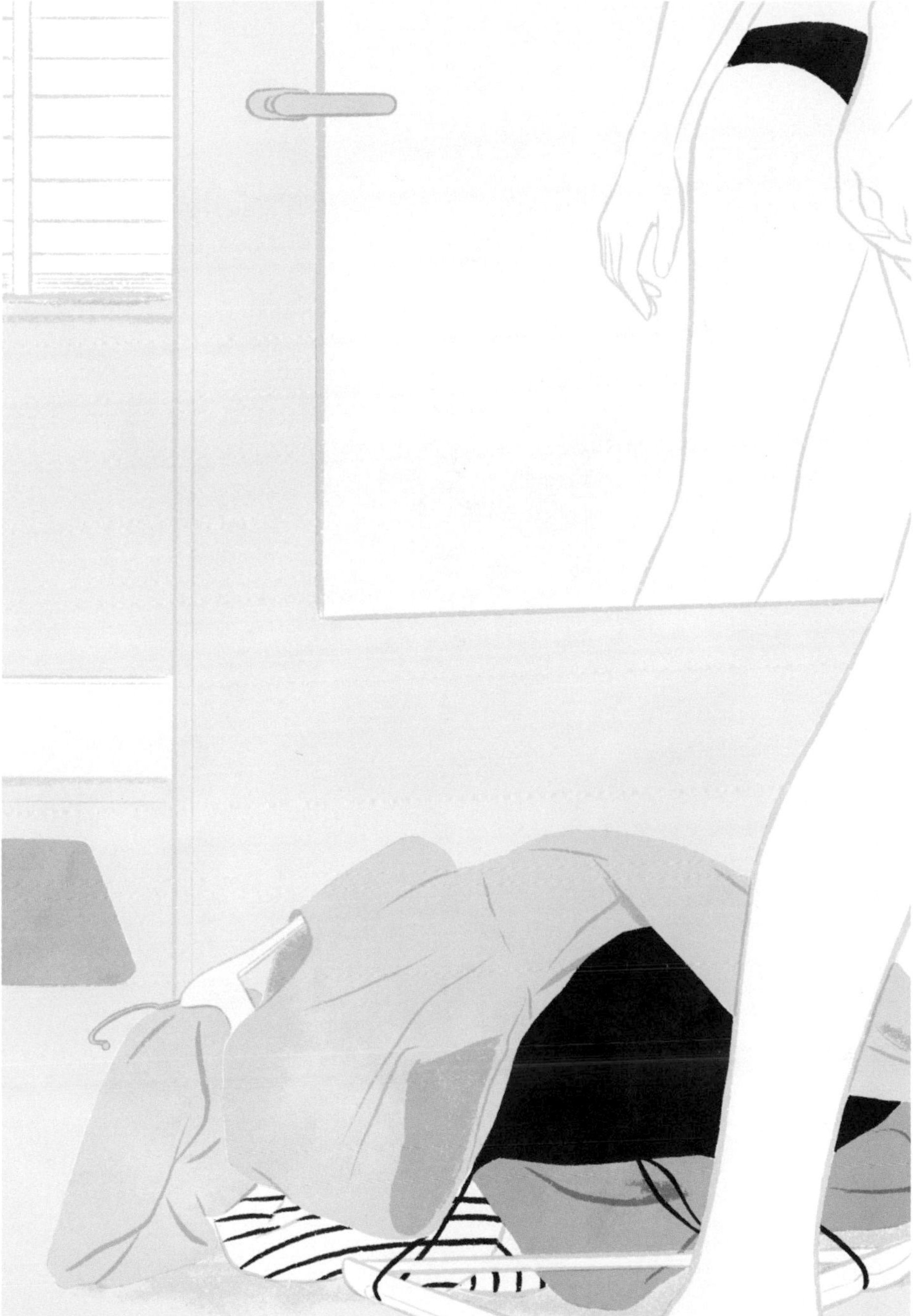

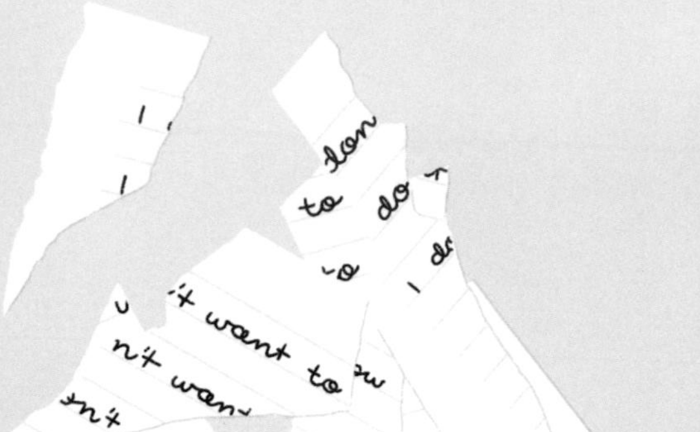

to
don
do
I do
n't want to
n't wan
n't

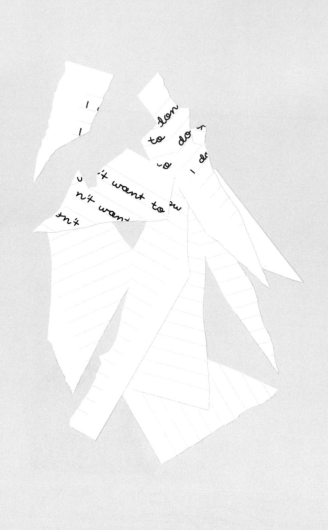

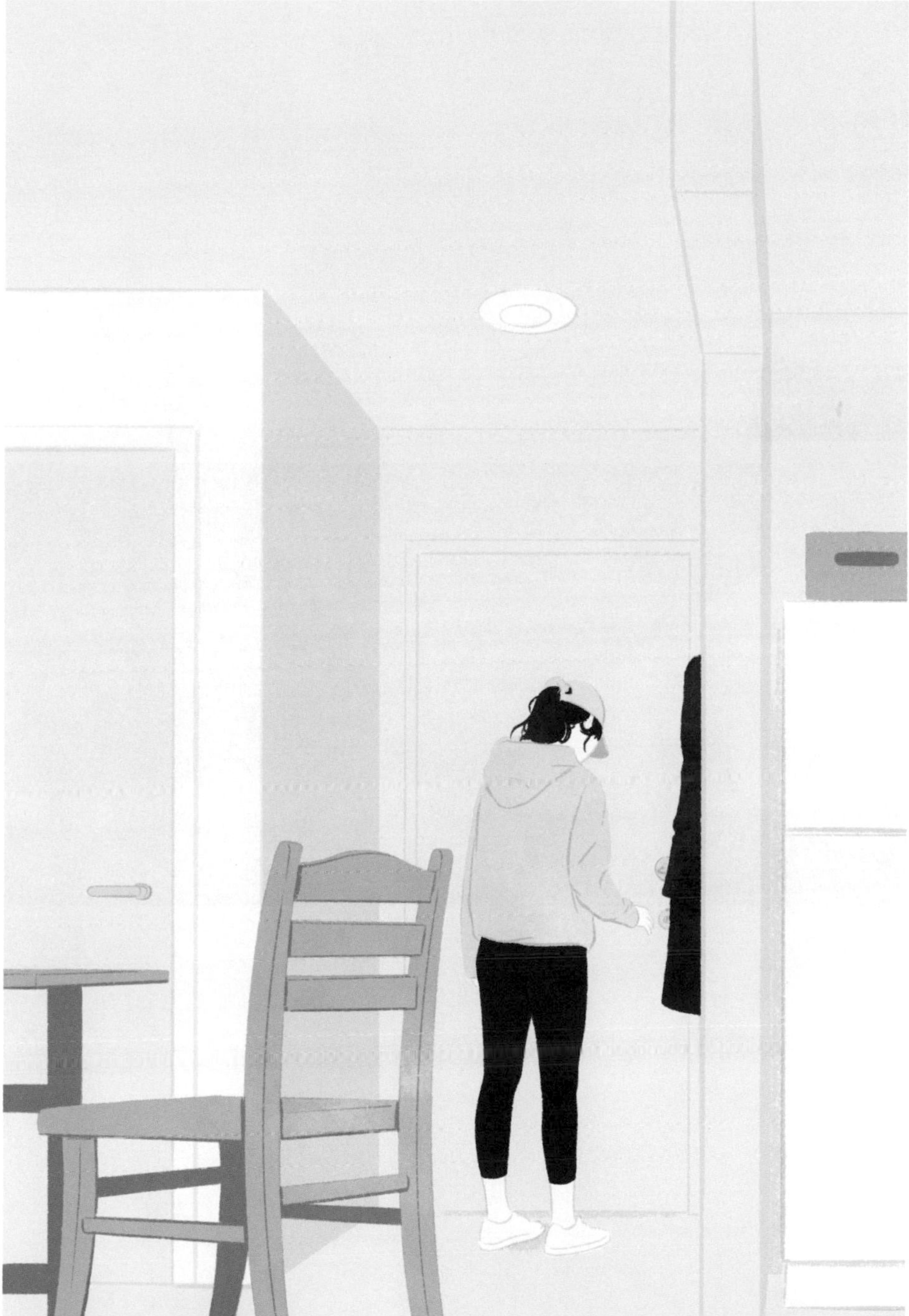

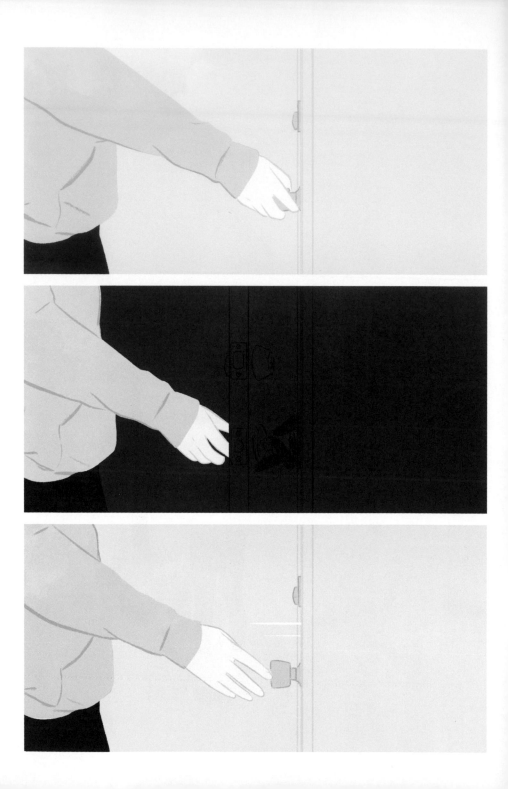

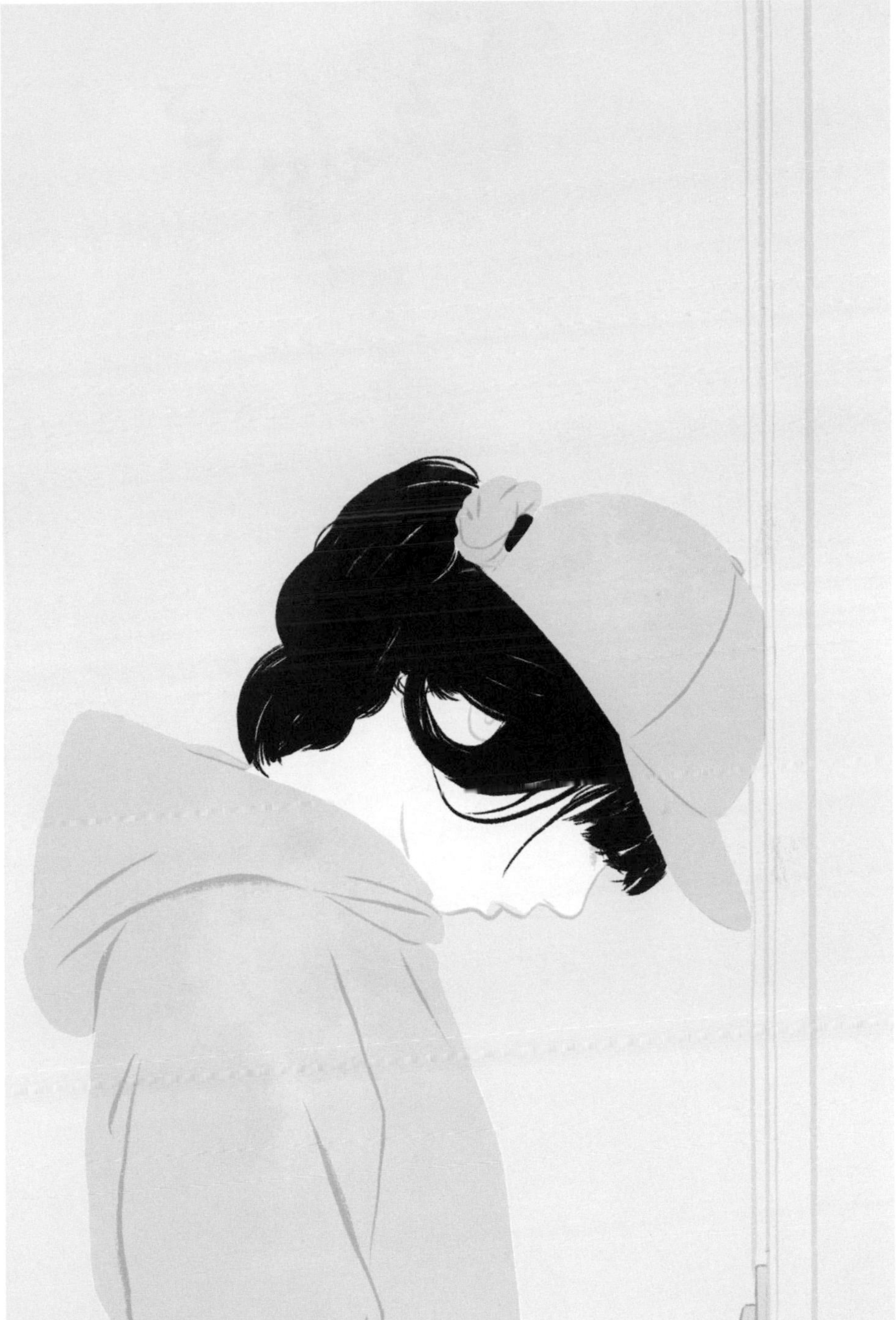

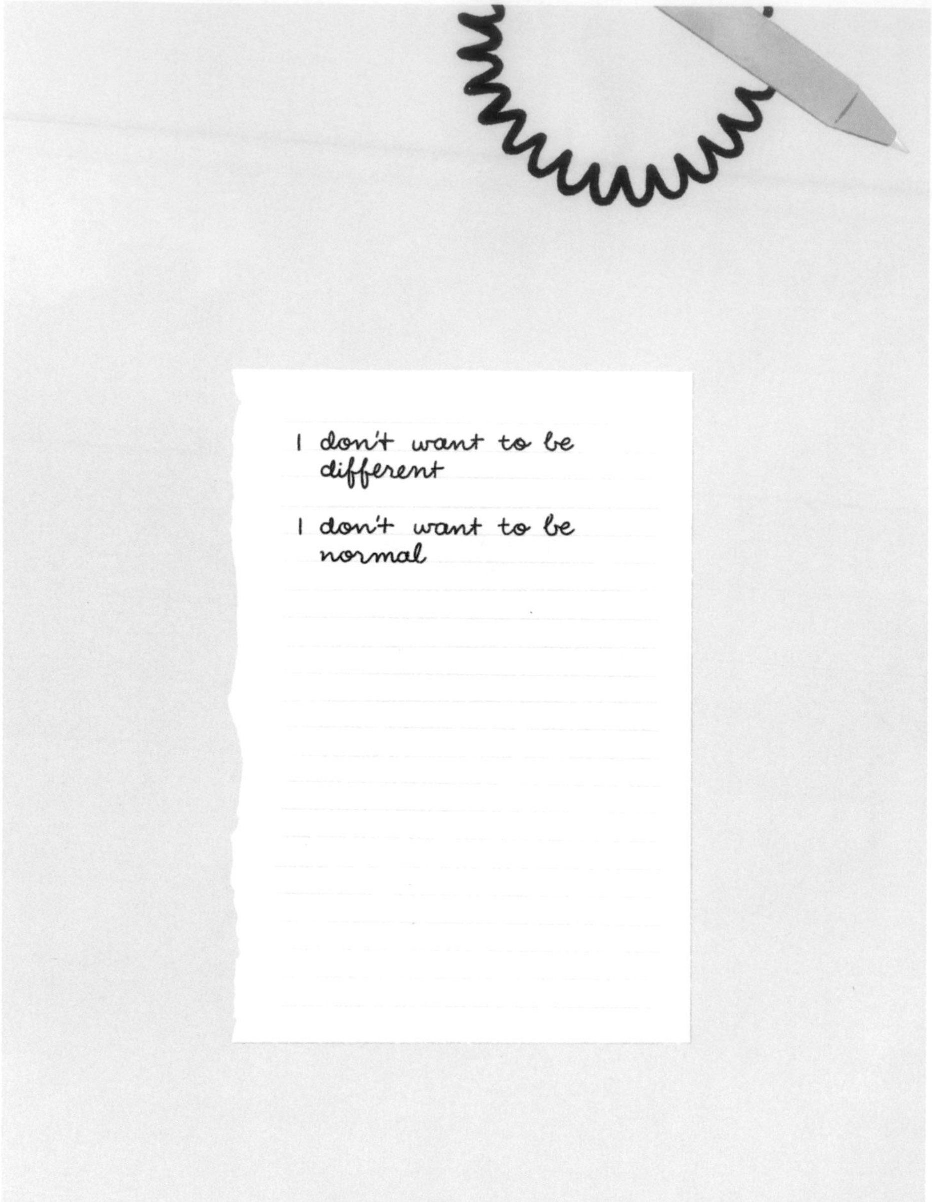
I don't want to be different
I don't want to be normal

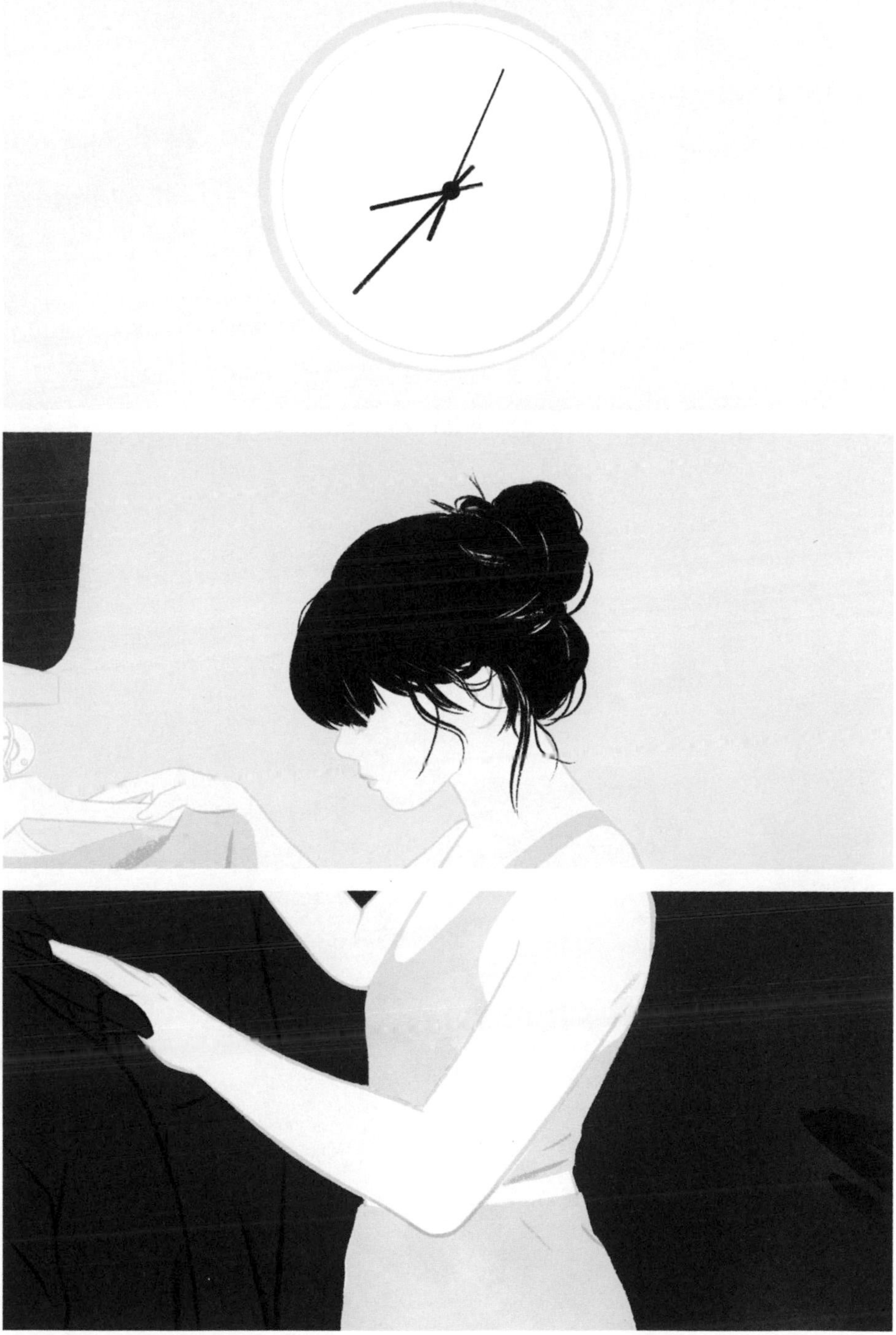

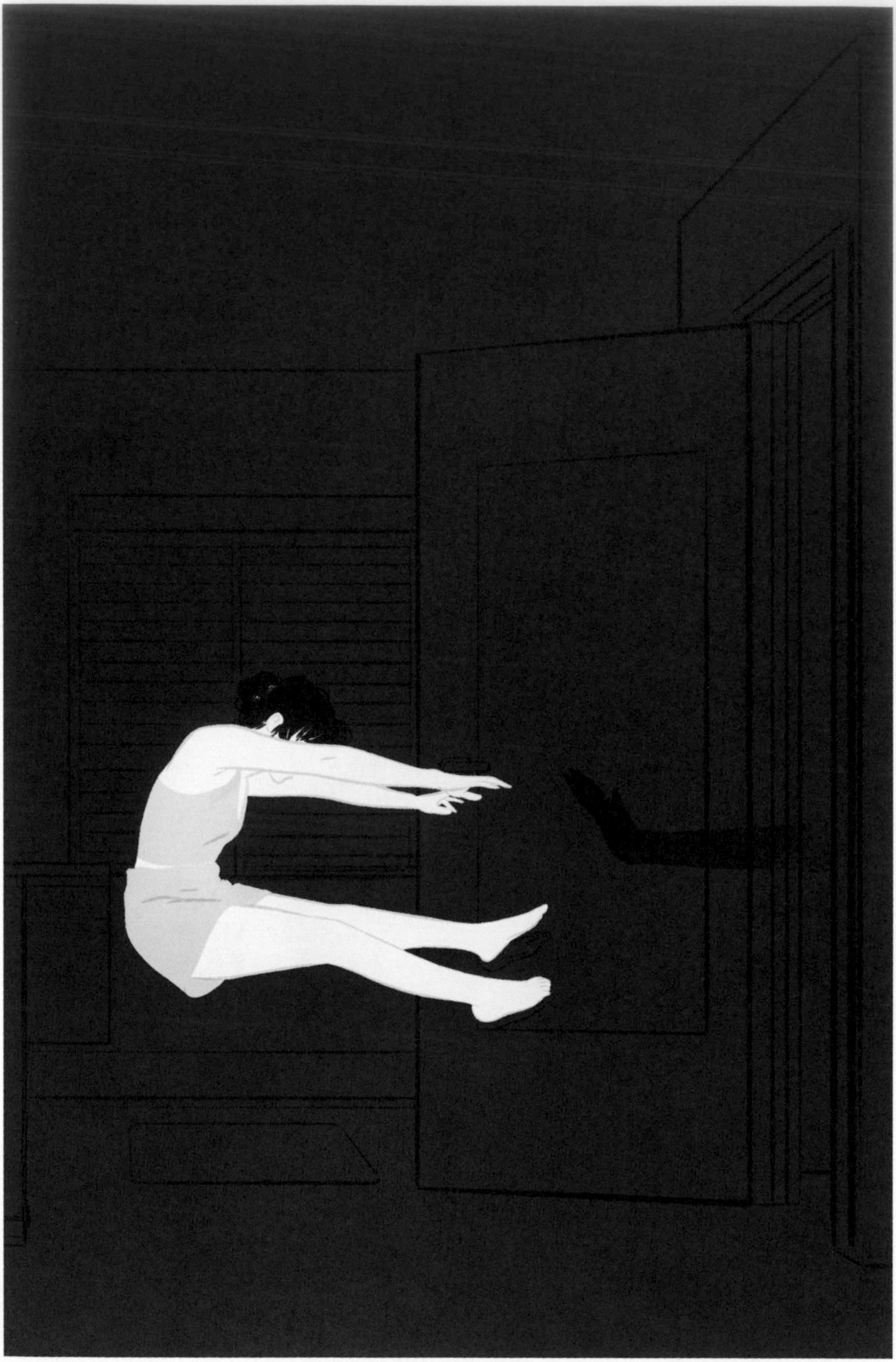

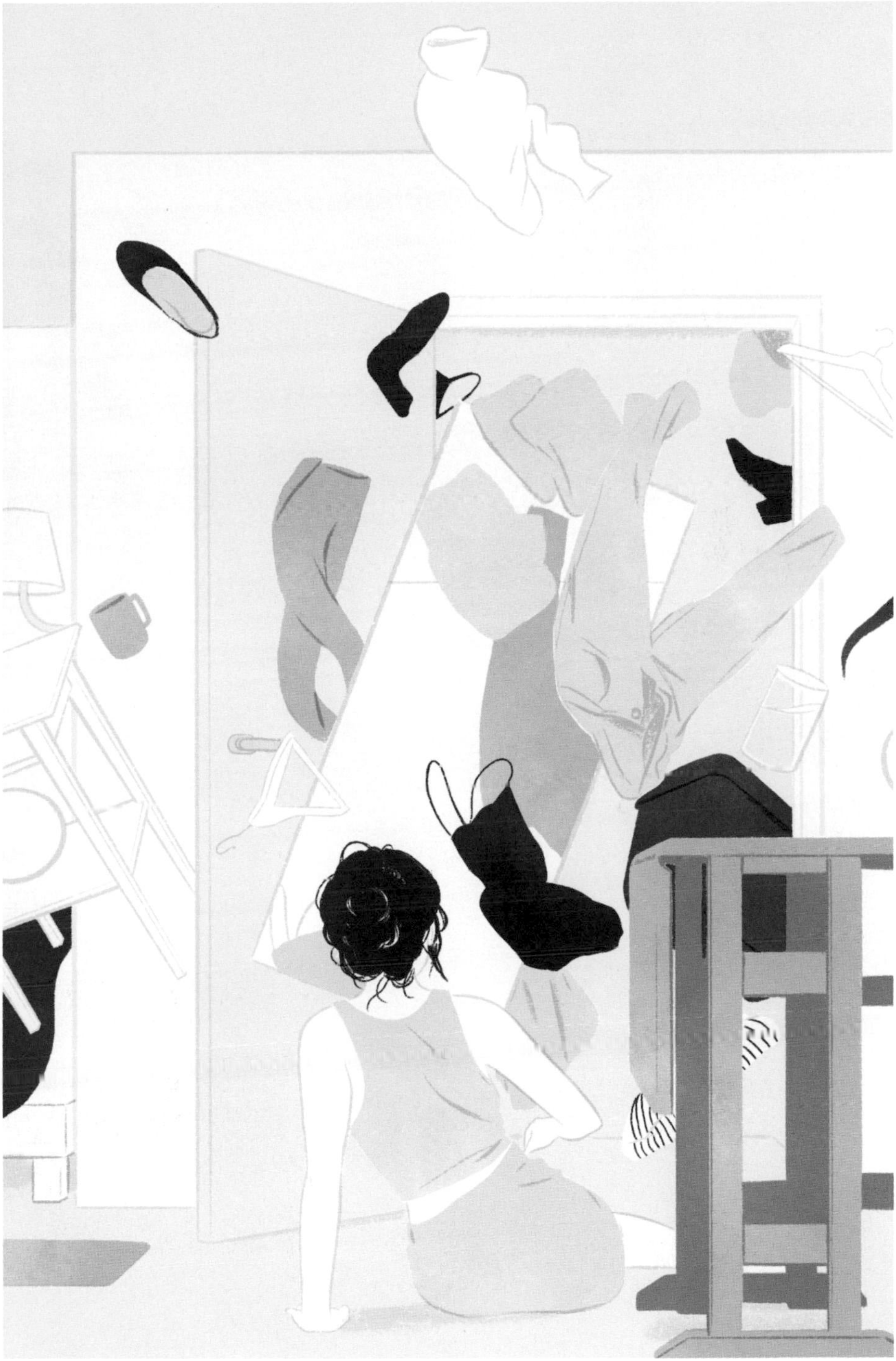

who are you?

what do you want?

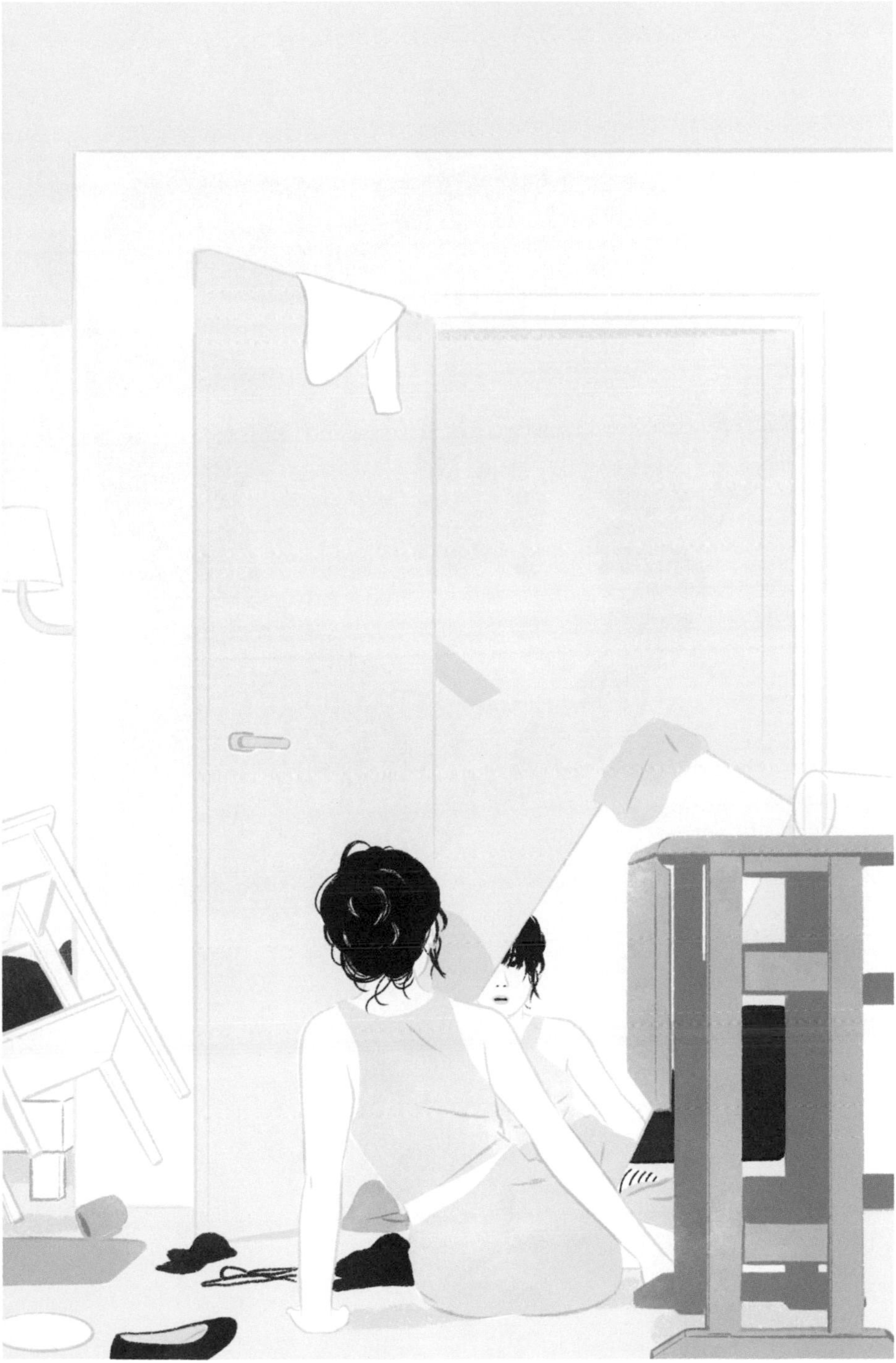

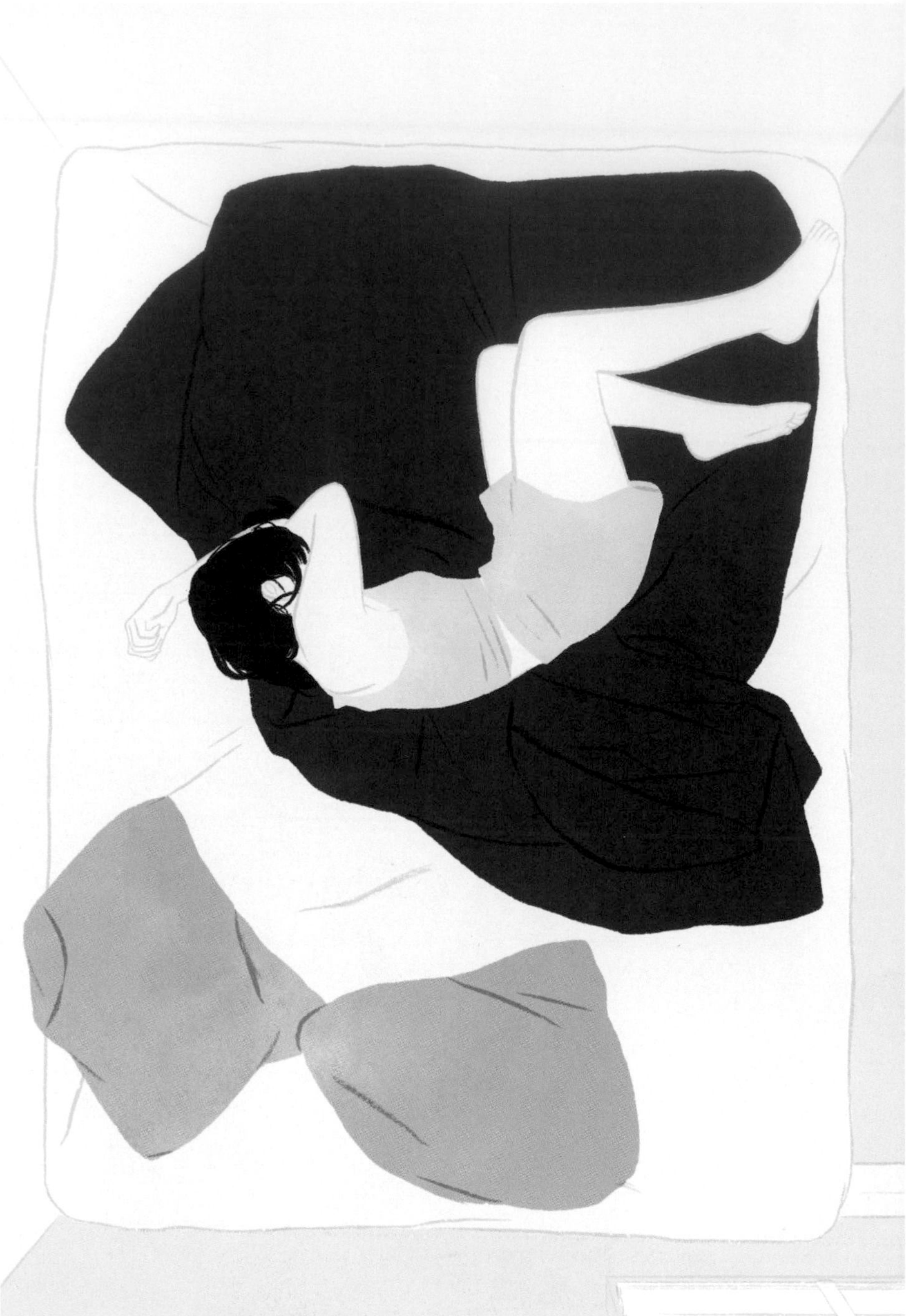

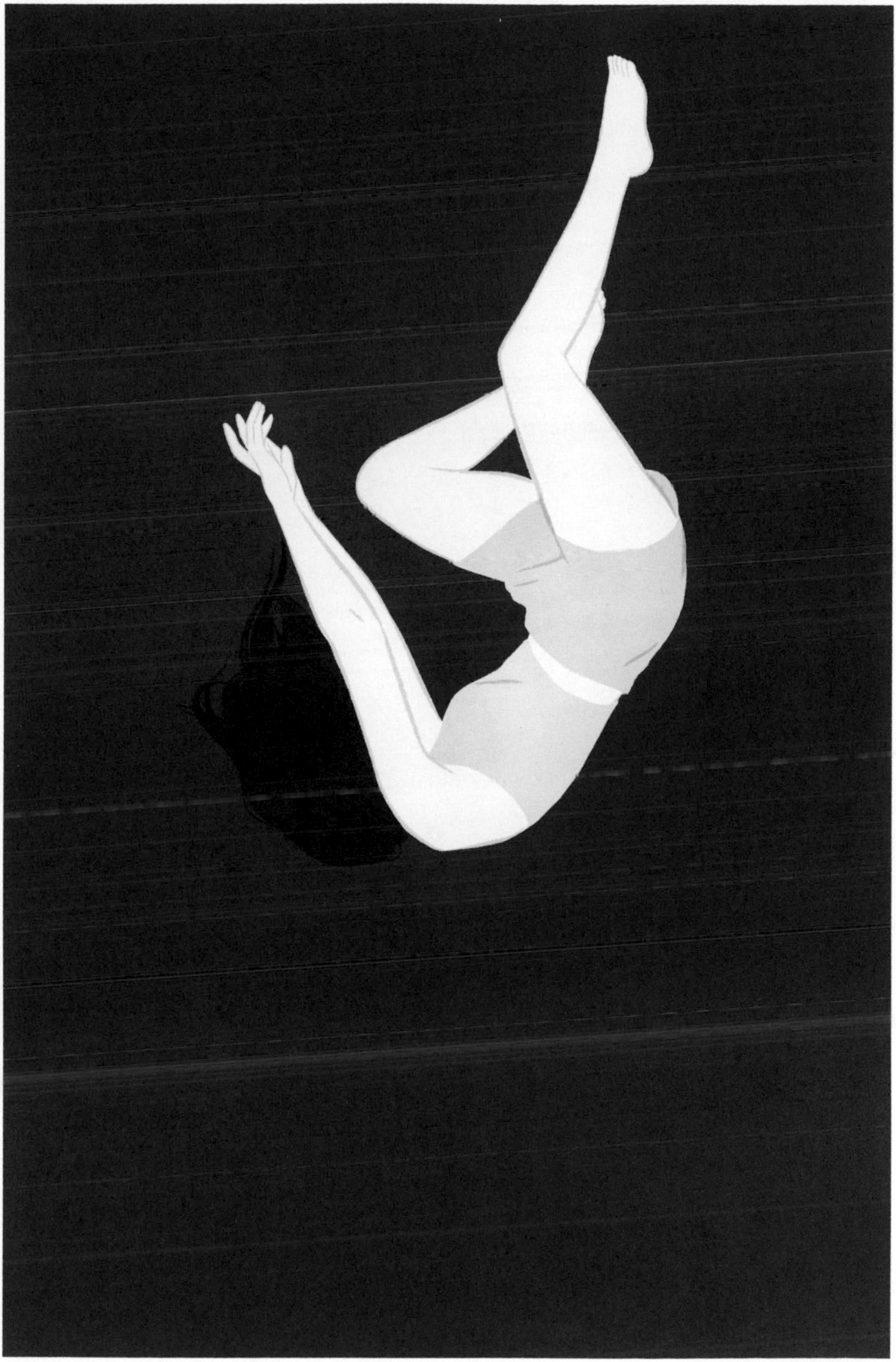

Constantly

3 1901 06144 5757